GW01366980

A CHRISTMAS TREASURY

HUTCHINSON
London Sydney Auckland Johannesburg

JANE YOLEN

ILLUSTRATIONS AND DECORATIONS BY
TOMIE dePAOLA

ORIGINAL MUSIC AND ARRANGEMENTS BY
ADAM STEMPLE

For Refna, Patti, and Margaret,
my book angels
—J Y

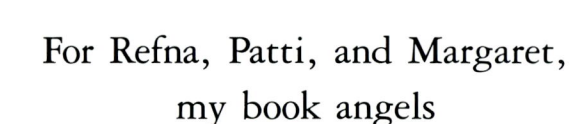

... AND MY DESIGNER ANGELS, GUNTA, PATRICK, +NANETTE.-T.deP.

Copyright © Text Jane Yolen 1991
Copyright © Illustrations Tomie dePaola 1991
Musical arrangements and original music copyright © 1991 by Adam Stemple
The rights of Jane Yolen and Tomie dePaola to be identified as the author
and illustrator of this work have been asserted by them in accordance
with the Copyright, Designs and Patents Act, 1988.
All rights reserved

First published in 1991 by G P Putnam's Sons, a division of the Putnam and Grosset Book Group, New York.
First published in Great Britain in 1991 by Hutchinson Children's Books
an imprint of the Random Century Group Ltd, 20 Vauxhall Bridge Road, London, SW1V 2SA
Random Century Australia (Pty) Ltd, 20 Alfred Street, Milsons Point, Sydney, NSW 2061, Australia
Random Century New Zealand Ltd, PO Box 40-086, Glenfield, Auckland 10, New Zealand
Random Century South Africa (Pty) Ltd, PO Box 337, Bergvlei, 2012, South Africa

Designed by Nanette Stevenson. Lettering by David Gatti.
Printed in Hong Kong by South China Printing Co (1988) Ltd
British Library Cataloguing in Publication Data is available.

ISBN 0 09 176416 5

Hark!

"Hark!" sang the angels,
Welcoming all
From lowly hut
And royal hall.

"Hark!" sang the doves,
The chicks, the cows,
The wrens and larks
Upon cold boughs,

The ox, the ass,
The horse, the ram,
The humpy camel,
Newborn lamb.

"Hark!" they all sang,
And once again, "Hark!
For now the day
Outweighs the dark,

The world is turned,
And all to view
This holy child.
And *you* come, too."

Contents

And It Came to Pass . . . /9
A Brief Christmas History/10
The Twelve Days of Christmas/14
The Gift of the Littlest Shepherd/16
Counting Sheep/20
Come All Ye Shepherds/22
We Three Camels/24
We Three Kings of Orient Are/26
The Greedy Woman/28
Mary Had a Baby/37
Christmas Animals/38
The Praising Cows/42
The Littlest Camel/46
Carol of the Birds/50
The Legend of the Birds/52
The Stable Hymn/57
The Donkey's Song/59
Christmas Plants/60
O Christmas Tree/64
The Fir Tree/65
The First Christmas Tree/66

The Holly and the Ivy / 68
The Spider's Christmas Tree / 70
Yule Log / 71
The Legend of Rosemary / 73
Deck the Halls / 74
Christmas Food / 76
We Wish You a Merry Christmas / 80
The Dough and the Child / 82
Here We Come A-Wassailing / 84
The Paignton Christmas Pudding / 86
The Boar's Head Carol / 88
Twelve Pies / 89
Christmas Carols / 90
Hark! The Herald Angels Sing / 94
The Foolish Shepherd: A Play in Verse / 96
Angels From the Realms of Glory / 104
Singing Carols / 106
Angel Tunes / 108
I Heard the Bells on Christmas Day / 109
Santa Claus and Giving Gifts / 110
The North Pole Express / 114
Baboushka / 120
Jolly Old St Nicholas / 124
The Christmas Gift / 126
Santa Rides / 127
Index / 128

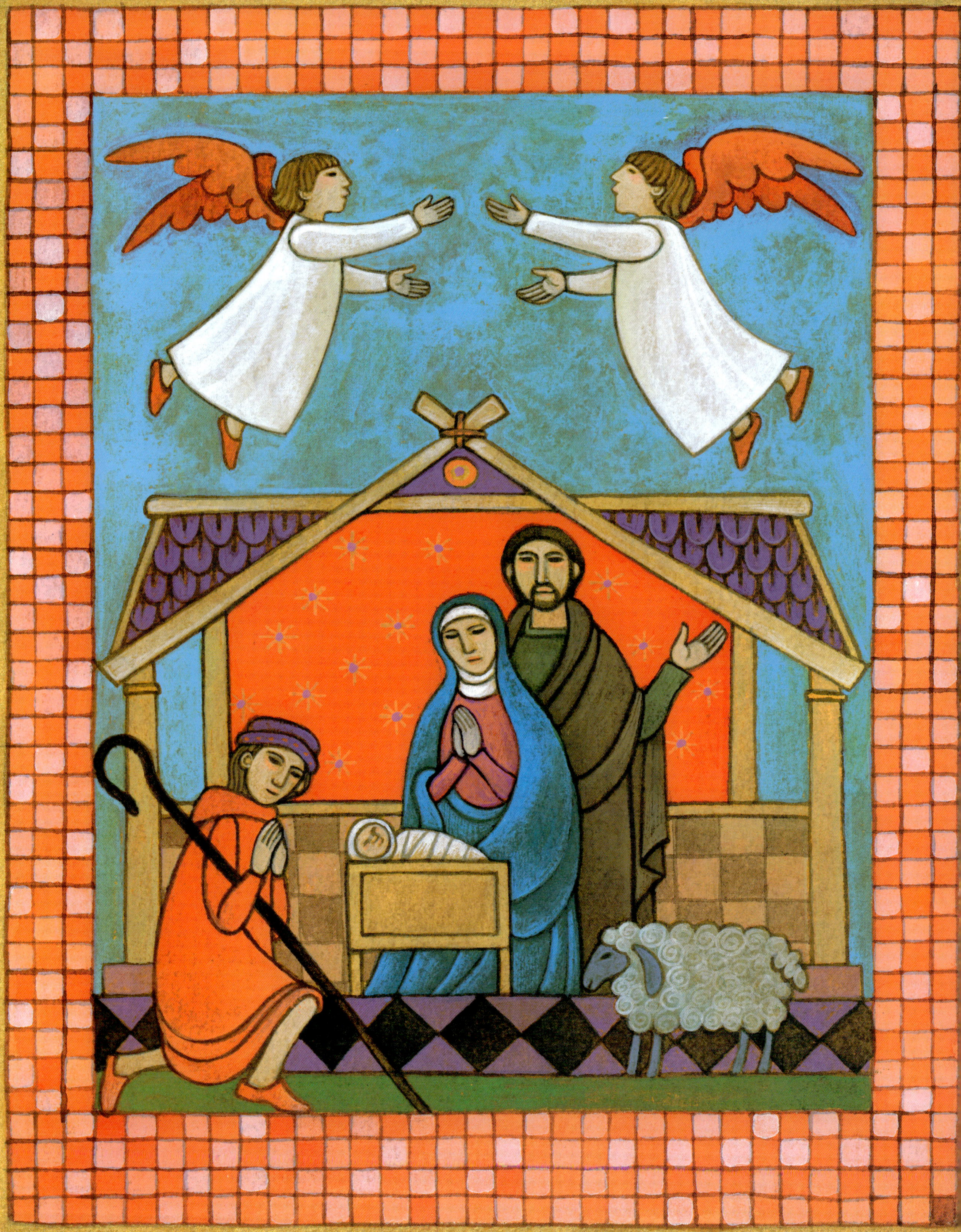

And It Came to Pass...

And it came to pass in those days that there went out a decree from Caesar Augustus, that all the world should be taxed. And all went to be taxed, every one into his own city. And Joseph also went up from Galilee, out of the city of Nazareth, into Judea, unto the city of David, which is called Bethlehem; (because he was of the house and lineage of David:) to be taxed with Mary his espoused wife, being great with child.

And so it was, that, while they were there, the days were accomplished that she should be delivered. And she brought forth her firstborn son, and wrapped him in swaddling clothes, and laid him in a manger; because there was no room for them in the inn.

And there was in the same country shepherds abiding in the field, keeping watch over their flock by night. And, lo, the angel of the Lord came upon them, and the glory of the Lord shone round about them, and they were sore afraid. And the angel said unto them, "Fear not: for, behold, I bring you good tidings of great joy, which shall be to all people. For unto you is born this day in the city of David a Saviour, which is Christ the Lord. And this shall be a sign unto you: Ye shall find the babe wrapped in swaddling clothes, lying in a manger." And suddenly there was with the angel a multitude of heavenly host praising God, and saying, "Glory to God in the highest, and on earth peace, good will towards men."

—*from the Gospel of St Luke*

A Brief Christmas History

"And she brought forth her firstborn son..."

The stories all say that Mary bore Jesus in the town of Bethlehem and that she laid him in a manger, but the Bible never gives the exact date of that momentous birth.

We celebrate Christmas, the day of Christ's birth, in the wintertime. Most people celebrate it on 25 December. But two thousand years ago the calendars were very different from the ones we have today. And at Bethlehem's little stable, no one was paying attention to that particular date.

The Armenian people celebrate Christmas on 6 January.

And the Latino people celebrate right through to 6 January.

Let's see—that's one...two...three ...four...

That's twelve days of Christmas—my kind of celebration!

Even before Christ's birth, though, the days around 25 December were considered special. The winter *solstice*, 22 December, was an important holy day for many of the world's people. It is the shortest day of the year, when the sun shines for the fewest hours, and there have always been festivals to "call back the sun".

The Norse celebrated with a Yule log and with evergreen decorations in their homes and places of worship. They held great banquets.

The Romans had their *Saturnalia*, worshipping the god Saturn. The festival included gift giving by the rich to the poor. At the *Saturnalia*, slaves were allowed to exchange clothing with their masters. Everyone ate and drank a lot.

The Gift of the Littlest Shepherd

It was the night the sky blazed with colour and angels flew down to earth, chivvying sheep and shepherds before them, that the littlest shepherd came to Bethlehem.

He walked slowly, well behind the rest. Not because he was tired, though his little legs ached with the effort of keeping up. And not because he was afraid. He walked slowly because the angels had told them they were to visit the newborn King of Kings and the littlest shepherd had no gift to give.

He did not have gold or silver as the three wise men had, presents fit for a king. Nor did he have their frankincense and myrrh to keep away the stable smells. He did not have gifts of woollen cloaks made of new fleece as had the other shepherds. Nor fresh breads or hot soup or the delicate little cakes that had been brought by the townsfolk.

But once at the stable, the littlest shepherd could not run and hide, for one of the angels put an angelic hand in the small of his back and shoved him inside. And there he was, kneeling by the manger, sandwiched in between a brindle cow and a spotted hog.

So the littlest shepherd reached into his leather pouch, the one strung about his neck, to see if he had anything that might serve as a gift. Anything at all. But all his fingers touched was his spinning top. He knew it was too old a hand-me-down to give a king. Still, he remembered how he often set it spinning to make his baby brother, Aaron, laugh.

Carefully he pulled the top out and wound the string about it. Only the brindle cow seemed to notice the motion. But when he put the top on the manger's edge and, with a flick of his wrist, set the top spinning, there was a sharp intake of breath throughout the stable.

The wise men shook their crowned heads. "That is not a proper gift for a king," they said.

The baby's father, Joseph, agreed, made a clicking sound to show his disapproval, tongue hard against the roof of his mouth.

All the shepherds and townsfolk agreed. "Take that dirty old thing from the child's crib."

But then the baby reached out his tiny hand and touched the top, which made it spin faster rather than slowing it down.

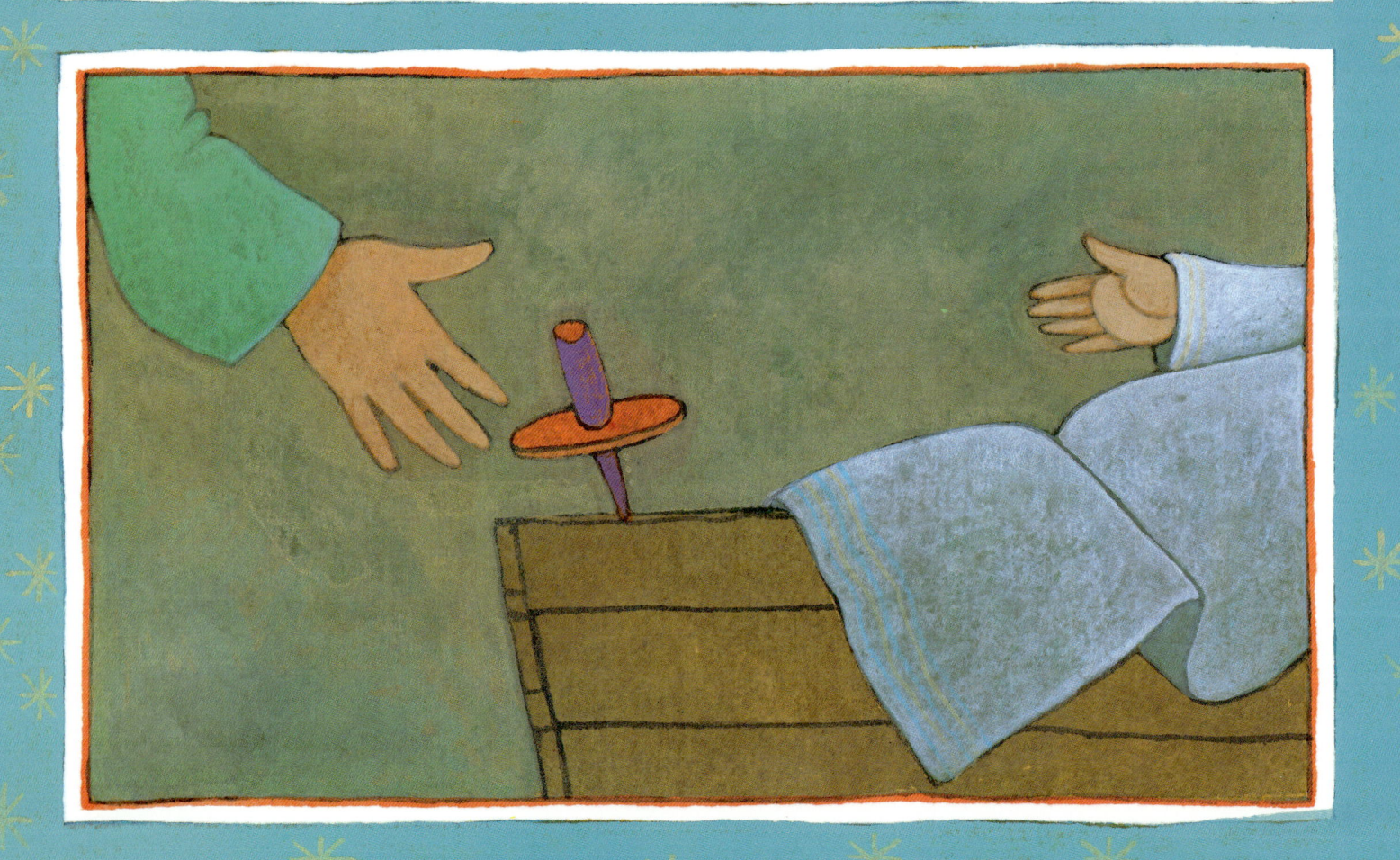

A miracle! thought the littlest shepherd.

Then the baby's mother, Mary, spoke above the sound of the whirring top, and everyone in the stable hushed to listen, wise men and shepherds, townsfolk and angels.

"You have each brought fine gifts, presents fit for a king. And we thank you for them, every one. But see—only the child has brought a gift fit for a child."

—JY

Counting Sheep

I am a poor shepherd.
Each sheep that lives the winter
is miracle enough for me.
That I have bread
and cheese and a skin
full of sweet wine on these cold hills
can pass for blessing.
So I will not say I was amazed
when angels thick as fleas
clustered in our meadow,
shouting hosannas that
frightened the sheep.
I lost two that night.
Still, a shepherd is not
so different from his flock.
We followed the bellwethers
to a rude manger
and crowded in amongst the cows.
What we saw then was miracle indeed:
a brand-new babe,
his unblemished face
shining in the light
of his mother's smile.

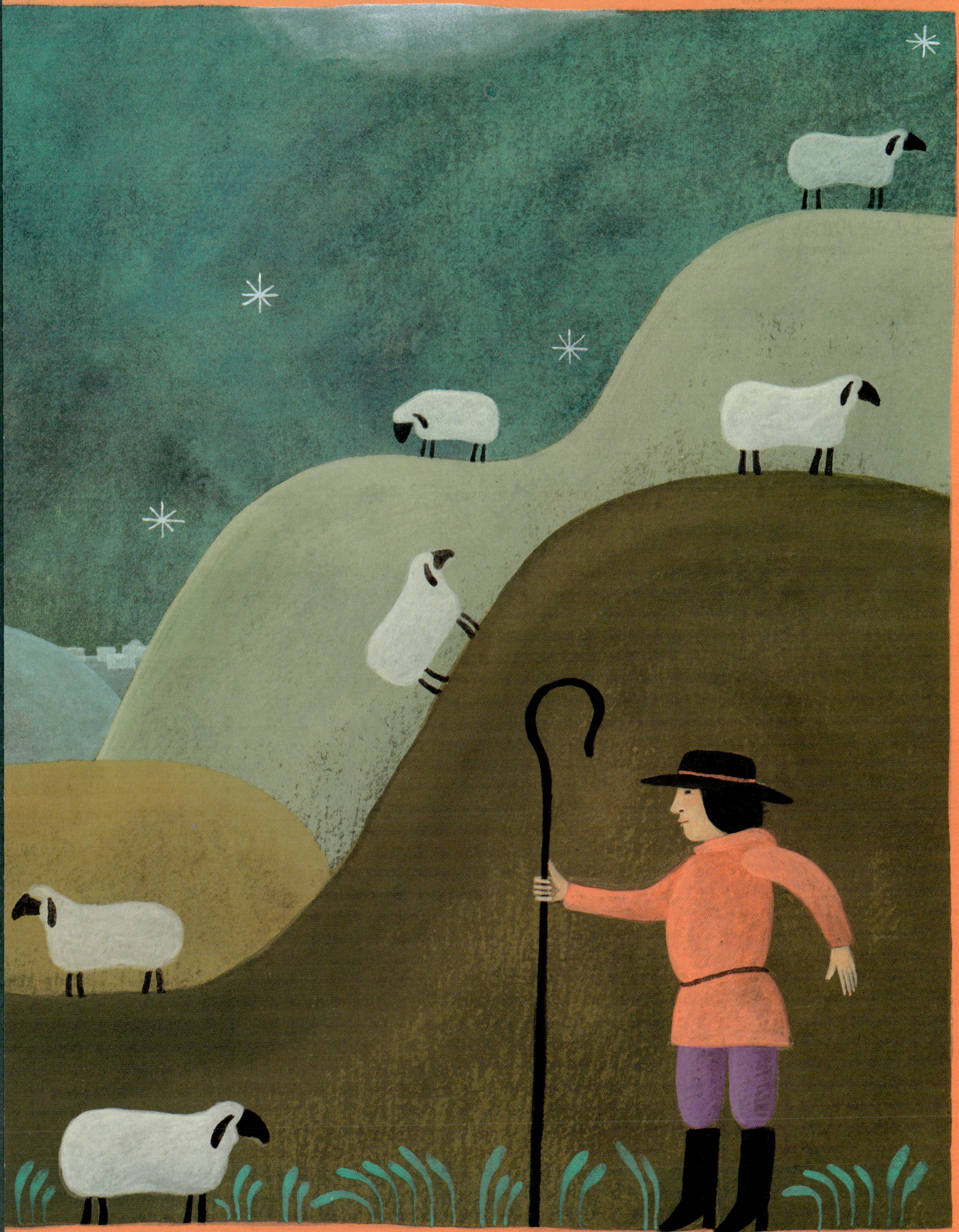

We Three Camels

I carried a king,
But not the Child,
Through desert storms
And winds so wild
The sands crept into
Every pack.
But never did
My king look back.
"Forward!" he cried,
"We follow the star,
We do not stop."
So here we are.

I carried a king,
But not the One,
Through searing heat
And blinding sun,
Through nights so cold
My nostrils froze,
And slaves wrapped cloths
About my toes.
But forward we went
Led by a star.
We did not stop,
So here we are.

I carried a king,
But not the Babe,
And also boxes
Jewel inlaid.
My packs were stuffed
With scents and spice,
The grandest ladies
To entice.
No ladies saw we,
But only a star.
We did not stop
So here we are.

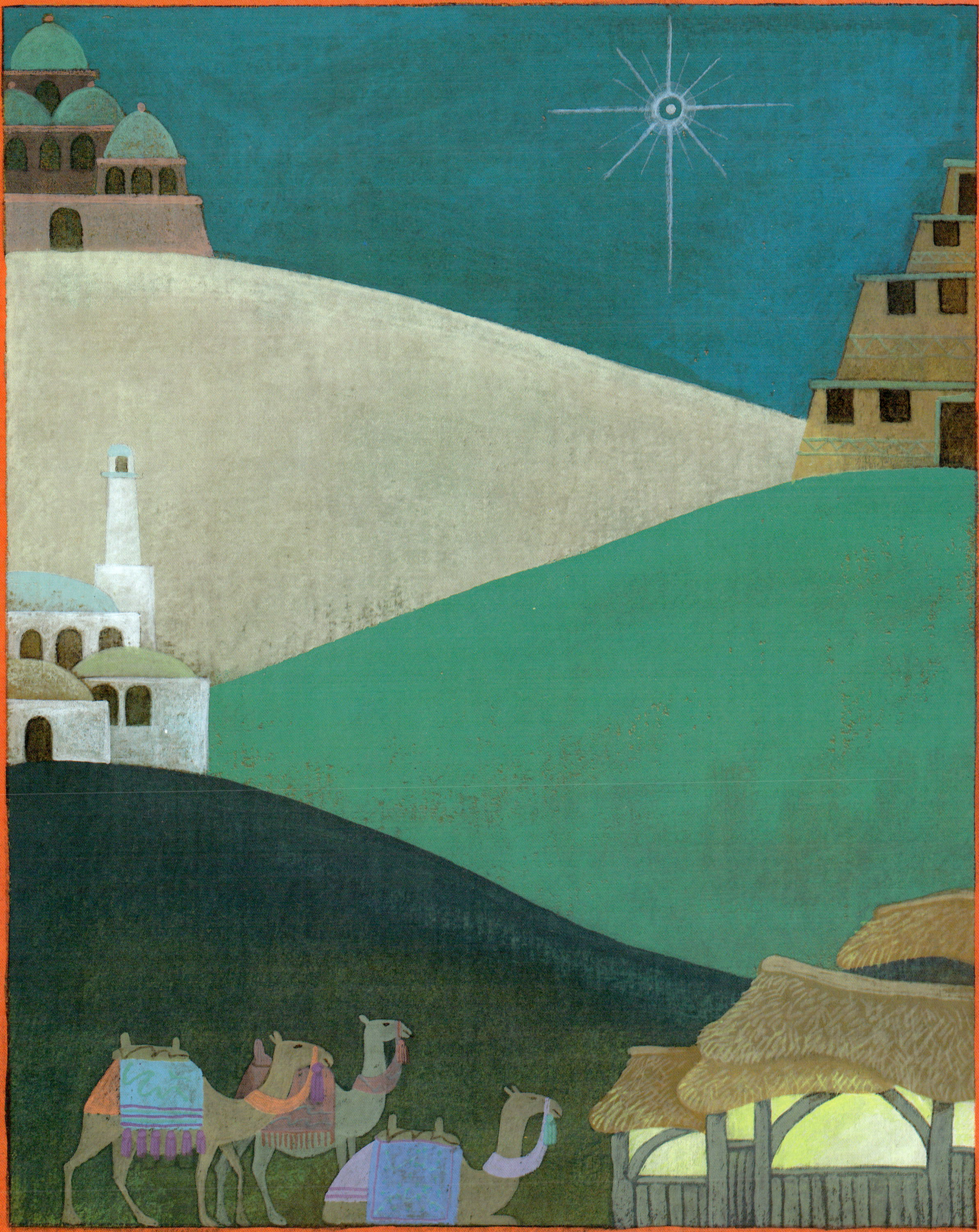

We Three Kings of Orient Are

John H Hopkins, Jr

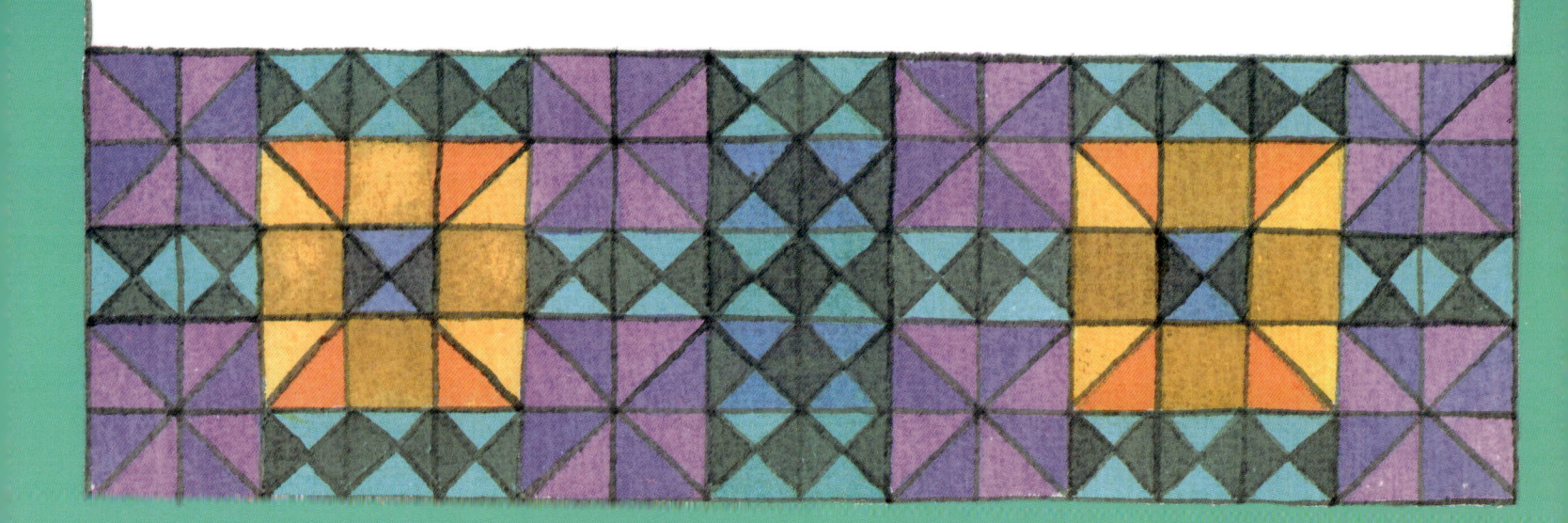

Mysteriously

1. We three kings of Or-i-ent are, Bear-ing gifts we tra-verse a-far, Field and foun-tain, Moor and moun-tain, Fol-low-ing yon-der star.
2. Born a King on Beth-le-hem's plain, Gold I bring to crown Him a-gain; King for-ev-er, ceas-ing nev-er Ov-er us all to reign.
3. Frank-in-cense to of-fer have I, In-cense owns a De-i-ty nigh; Pray'r and prais-ing, all men rais-ing, Wor-ship Him, God on high.

Chorus

O— star of wonder, star of night,
Star with royal beauty bright,
Westward leading, still proceeding,
Guide us to thy perfect light.

4. Myrrh is mine; its bitter perfume
   Breathes a life of gathering gloom;
   Sorrowing, sighing, bleeding, dying,
   Sealed in the stone-cold tomb.
   Chorus

5. Glorious now behold Him arise,
   King and God and sacrifice,
   Heaven sings "Hallelujah!"
   "Hallelujah!" earth replies.
   Chorus

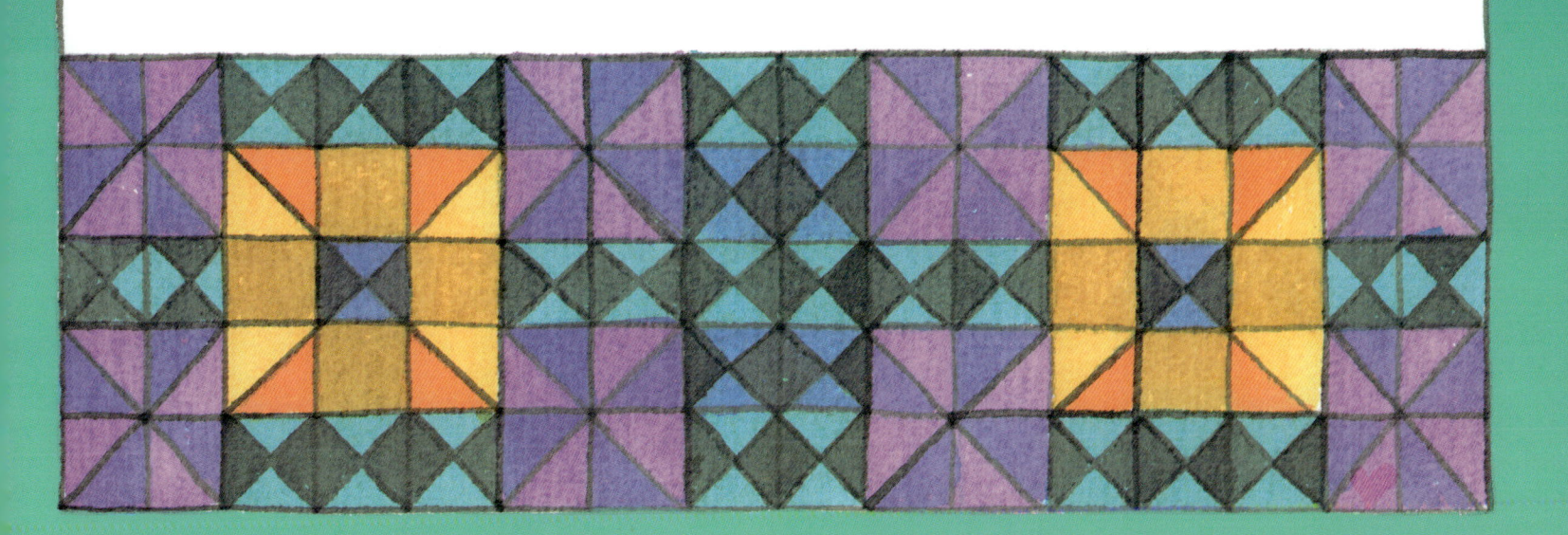

The Greedy Woman

The Holy Family had to flee the little stable in Bethlehem, for Herod's troops were searching for all new babies, with orders to kill them. And so the Holy Family travelled day after wearying day, sheltering in houses and in hovels and in barns.

At last, late one night, they came to a little village. The Babe was fretful and Mary so exhausted, Joseph had to steady her on the donkey's back.

All the houses in the village were dark except for two. One was an enormous house in the village centre, and every window shone with a bright candle. The other was a tiny cottage at the road's end. In a single window was a flickering lamp.

"Let us try the great house," Joseph said to Mary. "Surely there will be plenty of room."

Mary was too tired to remind him how there had been no room in Bethlehem. She just nodded her head and he urged the donkey on.

When they got to the front door and Joseph knocked, a woman flung it open. She was a big, blowsy woman with a scowl so permanent it had made lines in her forehead and lines like parentheses around her mouth.

"What do you want?" she asked. "Can't you see I have guests?"

"Shelter," Joseph said. "I seek shelter for my wife and new baby."

"Well find it somewhere else," said the woman. "This is no inn." She slammed the door.

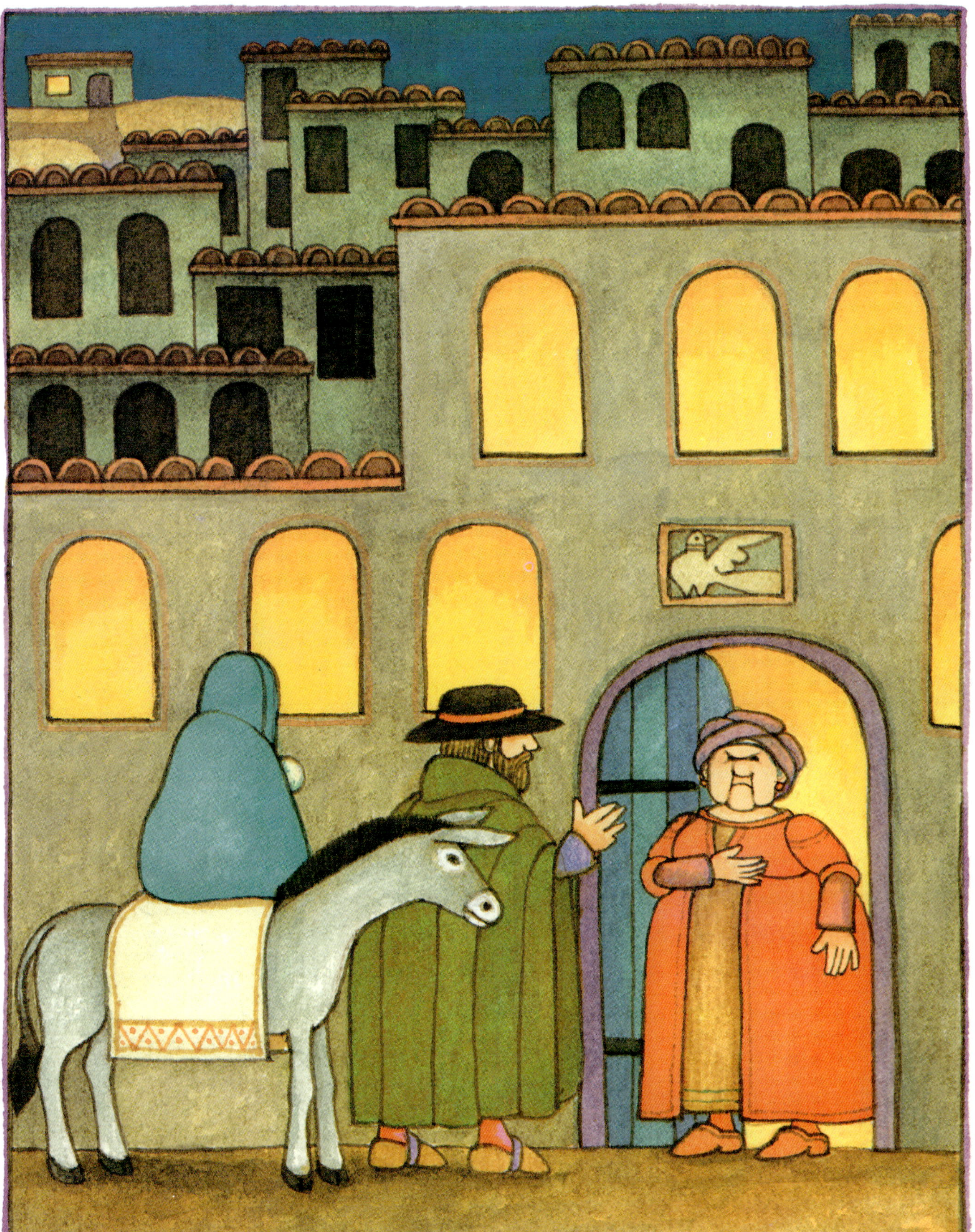

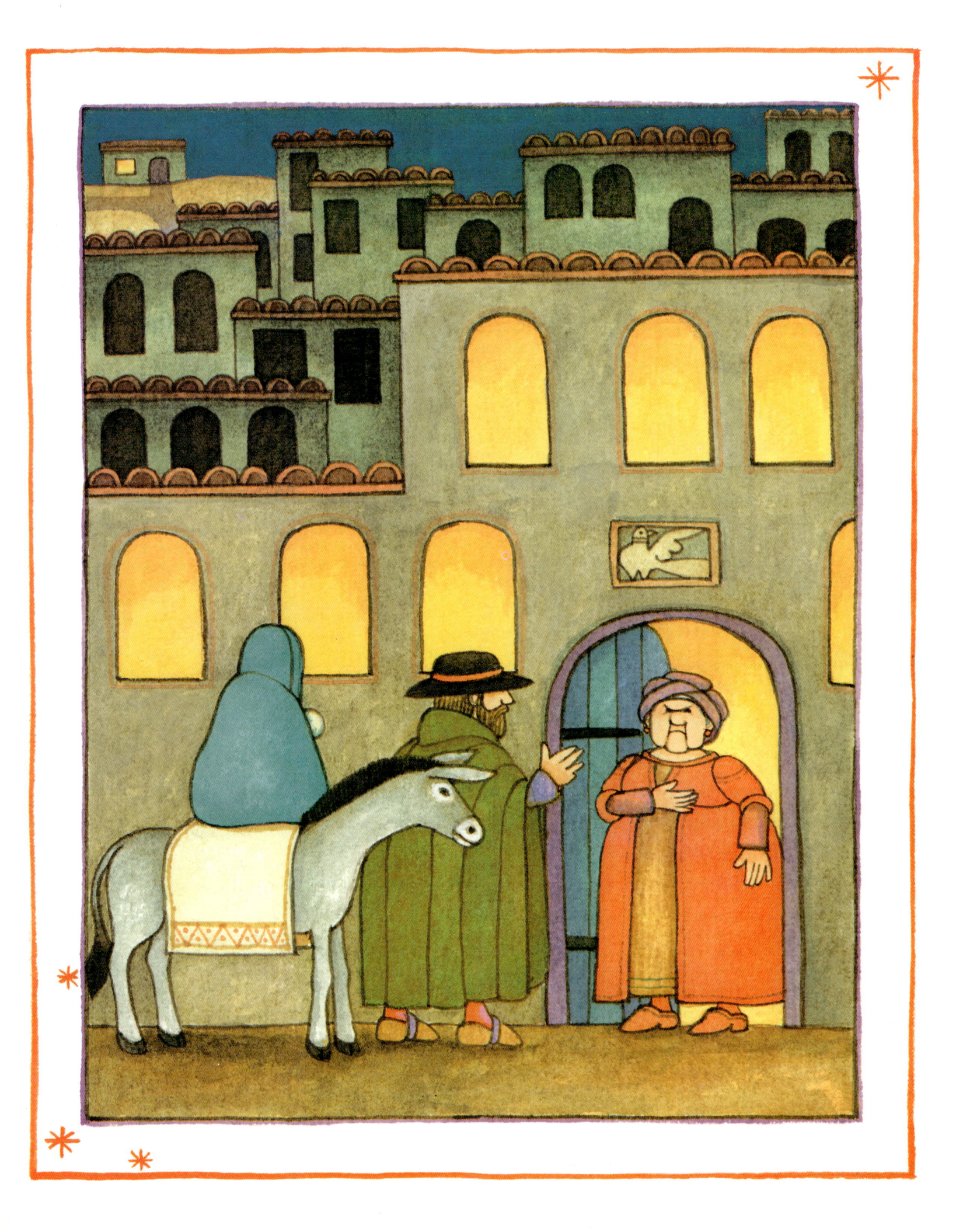

Joseph walked slowly back to the donkey, shaking his head.

"Never mind, husband," Mary said, holding the baby close. "Perhaps the little cottage will have room enough for such as we."

They rode on down the road and when Joseph knocked at the cottage door, it was opened by a woman who was small and neat with a ready smile.

"Come right in," said the woman. "It is too late and too dark and too cold for a new baby to be on the road."

And though there was scarcely anything inside the cottage but a bed and a spinning wheel, she welcomed them. As soon as she had settled them down in the one bed, she returned to her wheel.

"I am a poor widow," she said. "Your coming here is a perfect excuse for me to work the night through."

In the morning, after the widow had shared her meagre breakfast with them, the Holy Family made ready to depart.

In the door Mary turned. "We thank you for your kindness. And whatever wish you make first today, that you will have."

The widow smiled at such an odd thank you and waved them down the road. Then she turned to her work, all thoughts of the travellers gone from her mind. "Oh," she mumbled, "more work waits. If only I could spin the finest yarn in the world. How I wish I could." She wiped her eyes and sat down once again at her wheel.

But no sooner had she begun to spin than a glow seemed to cover the wheel, and as she spun, the woollen thread came out softer and finer than any she had seen in all her life. She spun all that day, never tiring. And on the next market day, she got a steep price for her work. Day after day she spun beautiful wool yarn and soon she was a rich woman.

Now all that time the woman in the great house watched her neighbour with a greedy heart. The lines around her mouth and forehead grew deeper still. She could not understand why the widow should have become so rich. At last she determined that she would speak to her.

One market day, she stopped at the widow's stall. "How come you by such riches?" asked the greedy woman. "How spin you such a fine thread?"

The widow had never been asked this question before, but she was not one for secrets, and she told her greedy neighbour all about the travellers and their thanks.

The greedy woman was furious, though curiously she was not angry with herself but with her lucky neighbour. She thought how luck had slipped through her own fingers day after day while fine yarn slipped through the widow's, but she did not know what to do.

Now several years later, the Holy Family returned from Egypt where they had fled, and passed along the same route they had used in their flight.

It happened that the greedy woman was standing at the village well and recognized them at once, so fine a portrait had anger etched in her memory. She ran up to them and cried out: "I am so glad you have come back! I meant to have you stay that night with me, even though my guests were many, but when I opened the door again, you were gone. Stay with me tonight."

"It is too early for us to stop," Joseph said, pointing at the sun. "It is but noon. We will go on a ways yet."

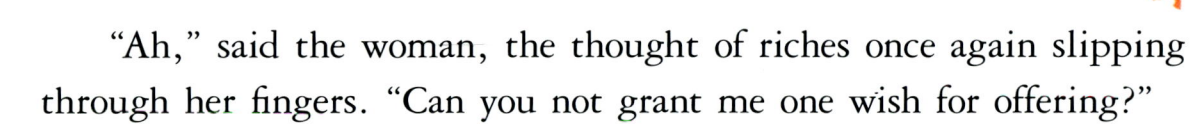

"Ah," said the woman, the thought of riches once again slipping through her fingers. "Can you not grant me one wish for offering?"

Mary looked carefully at the woman and on her lap little Jesus raised a finger up, but He did not say a word.

"Yes," Mary said at last, "you will be granted the very first wish you make."

The greedy woman did not even stop to thank them, but ran back to her house, slamming the door behind. She ran from one room to the next, looking around, thinking about her wish.

At last, tired out by all that running, she whispered, "I will think better with a cup of tea." But when she went to pour the water in the kettle, she remembered that she had left the water jug by the well.

"Oh, I am so forgetful," she cried. "I wish I had that jug right here."

With a great *whooooooosh* the jar flew in the window and settled itself down by her hand.

And *that* was the last of her wishes.

—*adapted from an Italian folk tale*

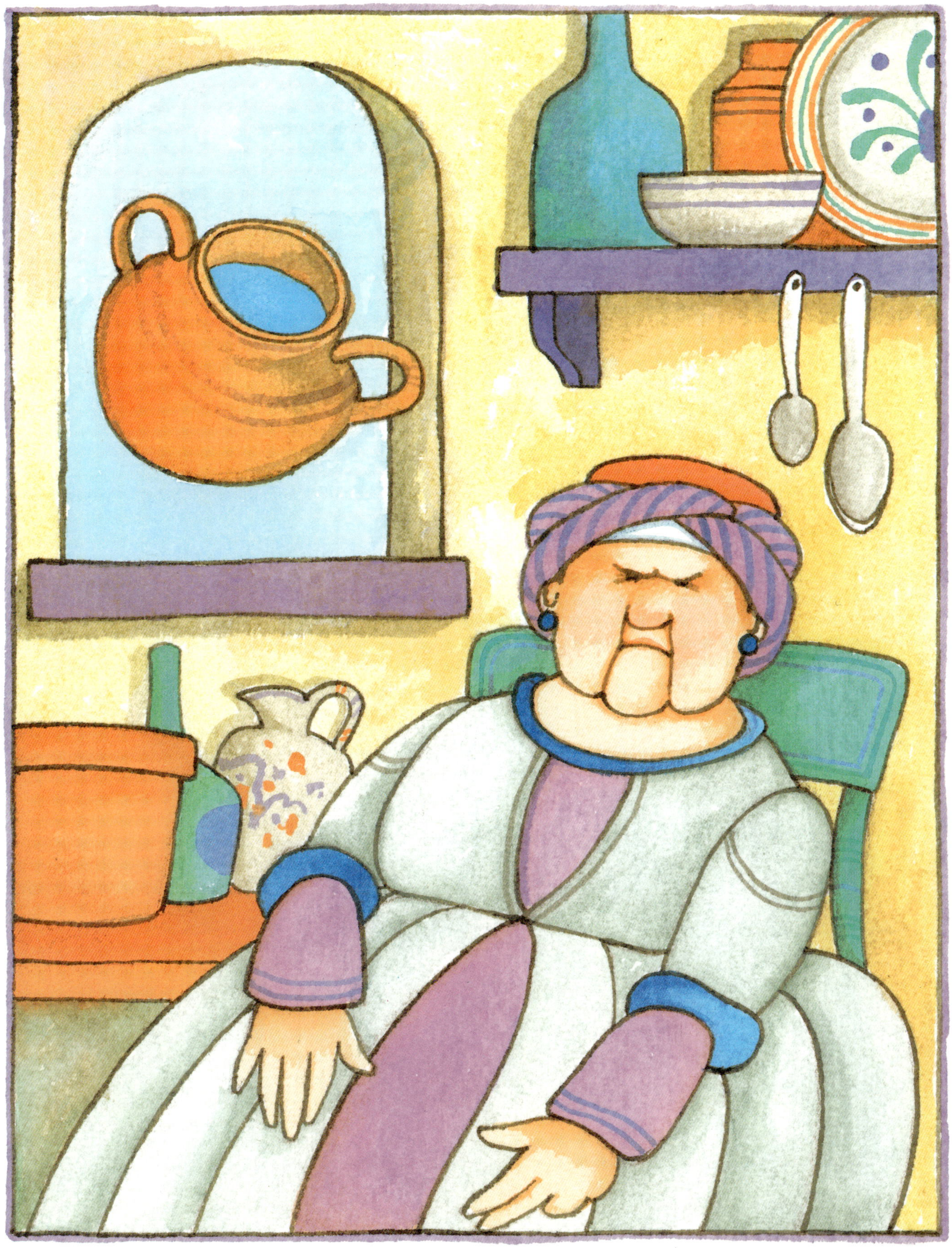

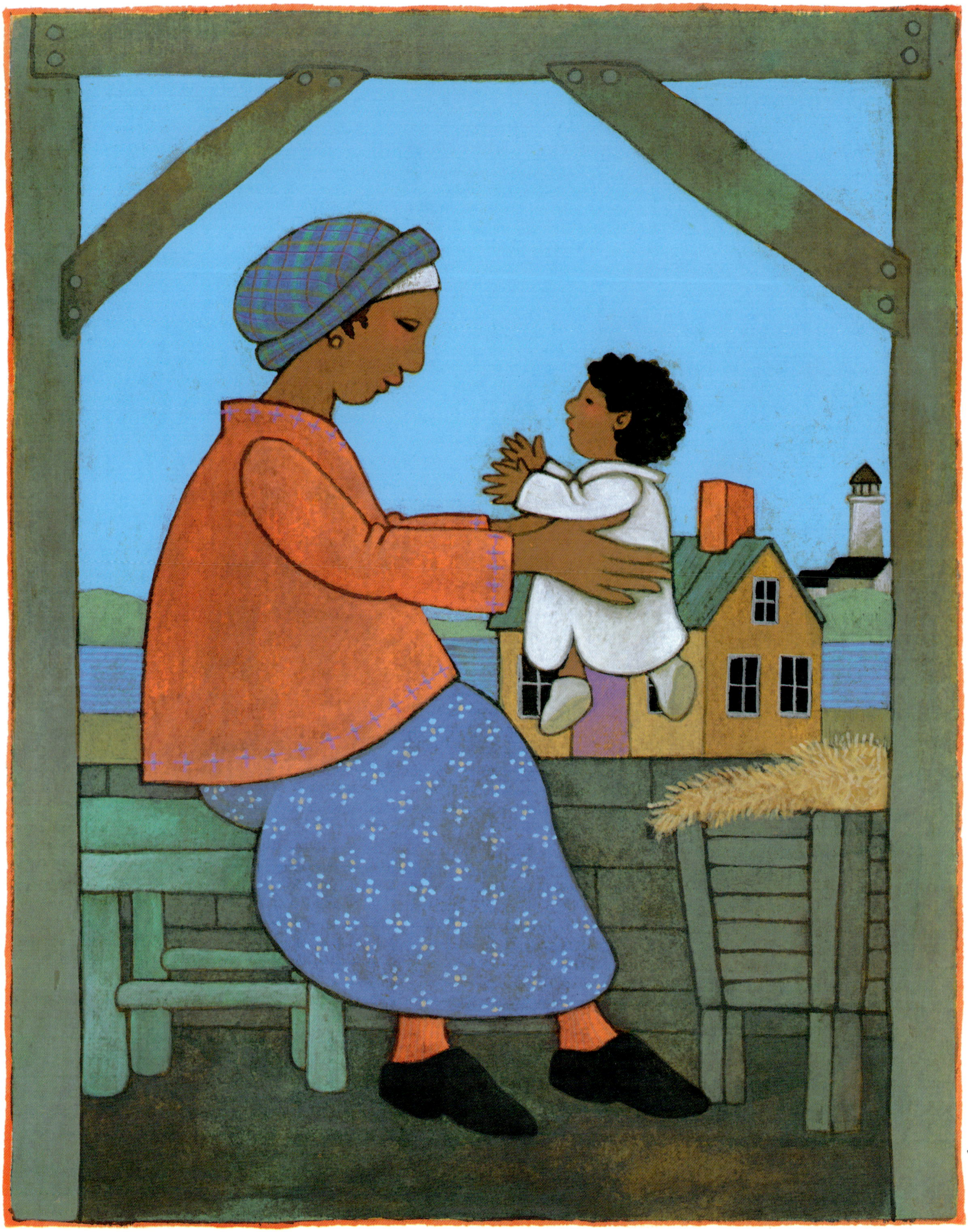

Mary Had a Baby

Traditional Georgia Sea Islands

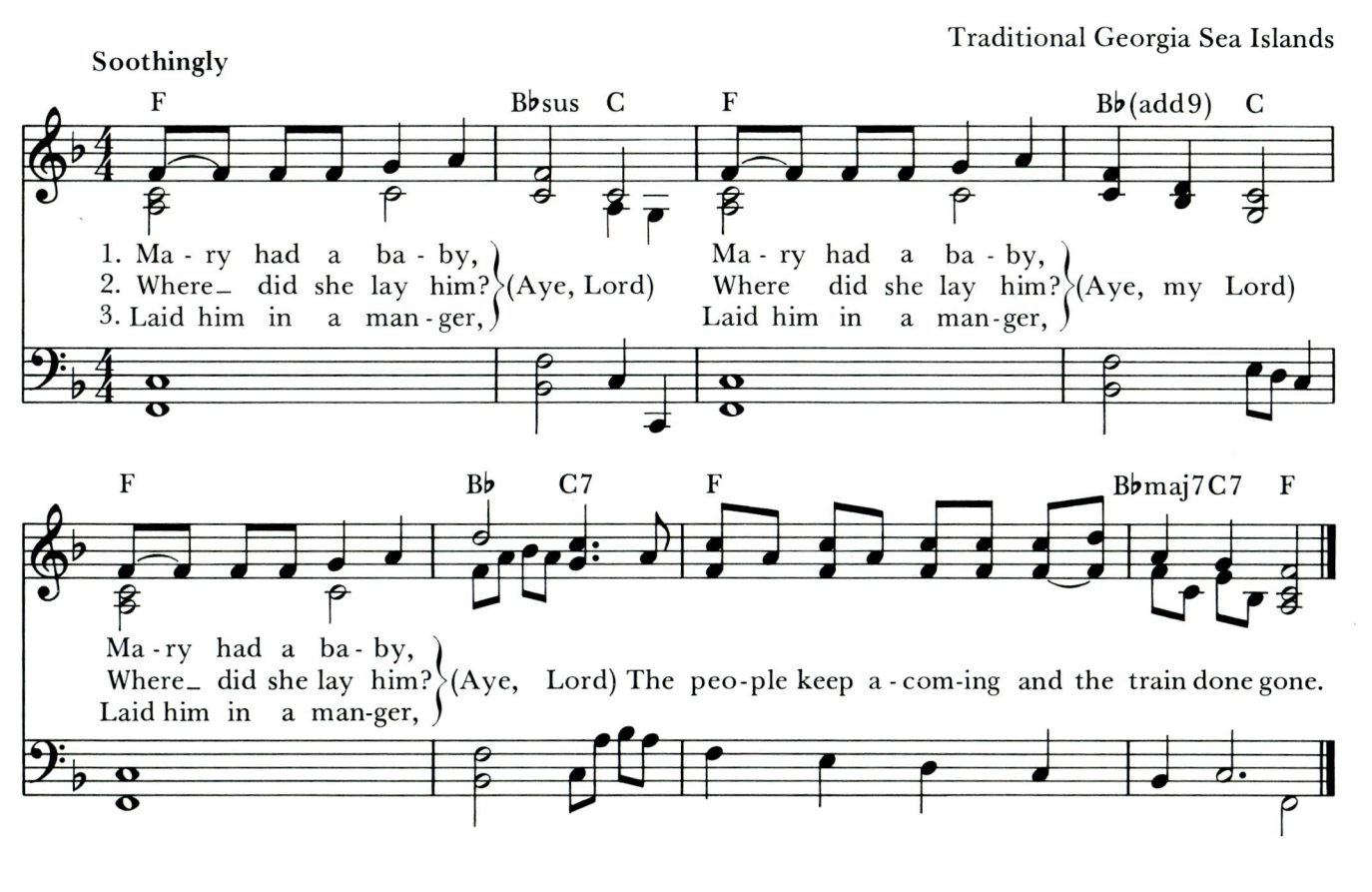

Soothingly

1. Mary had a baby, Mary had a baby, Mary had a baby, The people keep a-coming and the train done gone.
2. Where did she lay him? (Aye, Lord) Where did she lay him? (Aye, my Lord) Where did she lay him? (Aye, Lord) The people keep a-coming and the train done gone.
3. Laid him in a manger, Laid him in a manger, Laid him in a manger, The people keep a-coming and the train done gone.

4. What did she name him?
 (Aye, Lord)
 What did she name him?
 (Aye, my Lord)
 What did she name him?
 (Aye, Lord)
 The people keep a-coming
 and the train done gone.

5. Named him King Jesus,
 (Aye, Lord)
 Named him King Jesus,
 (Aye, my Lord)
 Named him King Jesus,
 (Aye, Lord)
 The people keep a-coming
 and the train done gone.

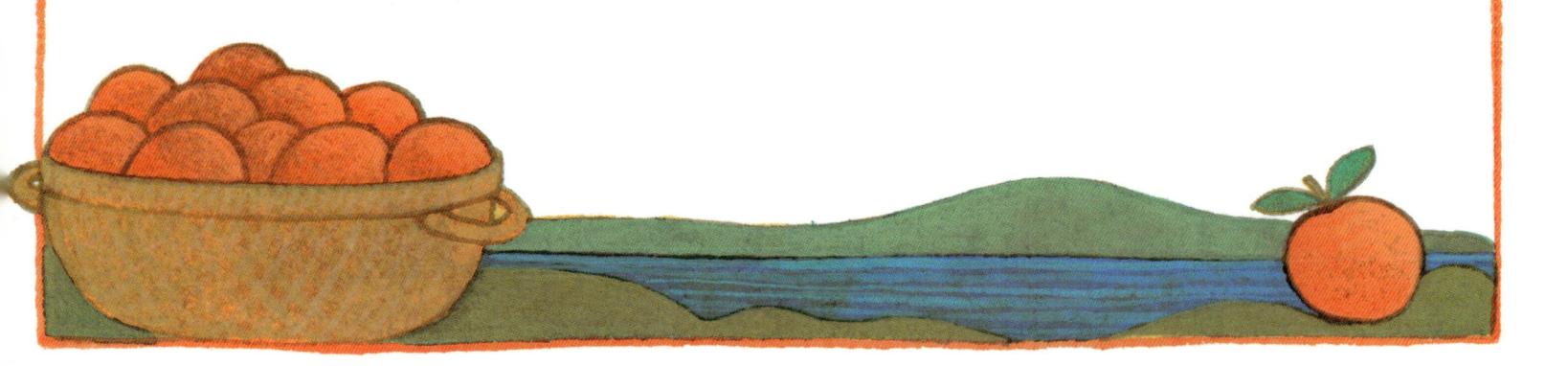

Christmas Animals

Cows, horses, and oxen were said to have warmed Baby Jesus with their breath, and because of it they are included in many Christmas celebrations.

In certain regions of Britain, the farm family crowds into the barn to drink toasts to the health of the animals. In some Polish farmsteads unleavened, or unrisen, bread is served to the horses and cows. Italian farmers and shepherds carry candles into their barns on Christmas Eve, bringing light to every dark corner. It is a custom in Norway to feed cows salt from a cowbell on Christmas Eve so they can find their way home at night.

In many European countries and in many of the American states, there are stories about farm animals being able to speak at midnight on Christmas Eve.

Bees were believed to buzz lullabies on Christmas Eve in parts of England. Even today some British beekeepers place a bit of holly on the hives in late December.

German settlers in Pennsylvania believed that the bees crawled outside their hives on Christmas Day no matter how cold the weather or how fast the snow fell.

Camels, called "ships of the desert", were what the three wise men rode as they followed the star in the East. Camels are still used today for desert transportation, and many Christmas legends, stories, and poems feature camels.

Goats play a large role in Scandinavian Christmas celebrations. In Sweden, the *Yul-bock*, or Yule ram, is said to butt any naughty children. To remind their children to be good, Swedish parents place a small straw goat in amongst the Christmas candles. In Norway, the Yule ram is called *Julebukk* and children leave out a dish of food for him on Christmas Eve. If the dish is empty the next day, it means good luck. If it is filled with grain, there will be a fine crop. In Denmark, the Yule ram is called *Klapper-bock* and he is a kind of hobbyhorse covered with goatskin and a ram's head made of paper or wood.

Donner and Blitzen are German words for thunder and lightning.

Then why not name the reindeer Thunder and Lightning?

They don't rhyme. That's called poetic license.

I didn't know Santa needed a licence to drive his sleigh.

Reindeer are newcomers to the Christmas legend. Before the nineteenth century, St Nicholas rode on a donkey or a white horse or even in a sky chariot pulled by great horses.

In 1821, an American poem titled "The Children's Friend" first introduced the idea of reindeer:

> Olde Santeclaus with much delight
> His reindeer drives this frosty night...

The next year, Bible scholar Clement Moore wrote a poem for his children called "A Visit from St Nicholas," and for the first time the reindeer—now grown to eight—were named: Dasher and Dancer, Prancer and Vixen, Comet and Cupid, Donner and Blitzen.

Rudolph the red-nosed reindeer was created in 1939 by Robert L May who wrote the verse that was published in a booklet. Ten years later, cowboy singing star Gene Autry recorded a song based on that verse. Rudolph has been considered Santa's ninth and most important reindeer ever since.

The Praising Cows

'Twas late at night on Christmas Eve
When we crept down the stair.
We passed right by the Christmas tree
With presents waiting there.

Outside the night was crisp and cold,
And Maisie said: "It's snowed."
We put on boots and both stepped out
Upon the moonlit road.

The barn door creaked and we slipped in
To listen to the moan
Of all the animals who thought
That they were quite alone.

I heard the cows both lowing loud.
The brindle bull did roar.
I put my fingers in my ears
And stayed right by the door.

But Maisie, she's a Christmas child,
Born smack on Christmas Eve.
She knows some things that others don't.
And this I true believe:

That Maisie heard the cows at prayer.
She heard them talk and sing.
She heard them praising hearth and home
And also Christ the King.

She stepped right up between the cows.
She gave the bull a pat.
And even Papa wouldn't try
To do a thing like that.

Then cows and bull and Maisie all
Fell down upon their knees.
And then the cock began to crow,
And buzzing went our bees.

And Jenny, our small donkey, brayed,
And Sam and Jeff both neighed,
And Pork the pig and all three goats,
They simultaneous prayed.

What could I do but also kneel
Upon that barnyard floor,
The cold, dark dirt beneath my legs,
And at my back the door.

And all the while the great church bell
Tolled midnight loud and clear.
A mighty star shone in the East,
And I thought God was near.

And then I woke up in my bed
With Maisie by my side.
"It's just a dream," I thought,
And then I almost—*almost*—cried.

But when I reached beside the bed,
There standing in a row
Were my red boots and Maisie's black.
And they were wet with snow.

The Littlest Camel

It happened that the vizier to three great kings visited a camel market and purchased many strong camels for a hasty trip. Among the camels he bought for his masters was a mother camel who was exceedingly strong of leg, but she had newly calved. The camel seller neglected to mention this small problem. And the vizier failed to notice it, for the littlest and newest camel was resting, still weak-legged and dewy-eyed, by a post.

When the price was paid and the camels rounded up for the caravan, the littlest camel went too, of course, following his mama. This time the vizier was too busy overseeing the packing of the saddlebags to notice the littlest camel. He was checking on the skins of fresh water and the packets of dates and nuts, the little honey cakes and the bags of dried olives. And he was counting the presents of silver and gold crowns and jewelled boxes filled with coins and sweet-smelling herbs.

The camels hawked and grunted and spat as camels always do. All except the littlest camel, who spent much of his time lying by his mama's side, drinking her milk. So each time the vizier looked over his masters' camels, he missed the littlest one.

When at last the caravan was ready, the littlest camel was lost behind all the bundles and bags. And when the camels swung awkwardly to their feet, complaining in that gruff camel voice, the littlest camel seemed but a shadow beneath his mother's great bulk. So it was not until they were deep into the desert, where the sandy dunes seemed high as mountains and the wind howled about them like a mad thing, that the vizier even noticed he was there. And then it was too late to send him back.

What a struggle the littlest camel had. Up the high dunes and down; up rocky slopes and over; stumbling and tumbling. His little legs could scarcely hold him up. But he could see his mama ahead and he would not be left behind.

At last the caravan arrived at a town. *Surely*, the littlest camel thought, *surely we shall rest now.*

But the caravan kept winding its way down the streets. Men and women and children came out of houses to watch and one time a boy shied a stone in their direction. It hit the littlest camel on the side of his head and he fell down to his knees on the hard-packed dirt. When he looked up, the caravan with his mama was almost out of sight.

He struggled up once more, afraid to lose her. But the dust of the caravan's passage stung his eyes, so he began to run with them half-closed into slits. That is how he failed to notice that the caravan had stopped in front of a stable at the road's end, and that everyone—vizier and kings and camel drivers and camels, too—was kneeling beside the road.

He ran right past, skidding to a halt in the stable itself and falling over in a tangle of dirty, bruised legs. This time he was so exhausted, he could only lie there moaning.

Then he felt a small hand touch his forehead. But when he opened his eyes, there was no one nearby. A voice spoke to him in his mind, a child's voice not any older than his own:

"Well done, littlest one. You came so far. And you never gave up. Because of that you shall be my ambassador to all the children of the world."

And so it is that every year, on the anniversary of that night, the littlest camel repeats his journey, going from house to house and leaving gifts for all the boys and girls. If the gifts are not as *fine* as those his mama and the other camels carried in the caravan, they are certainly as *good*, for they are carried with loving wishes from the Christ Child Himself.

—adapted from a Syrian legend

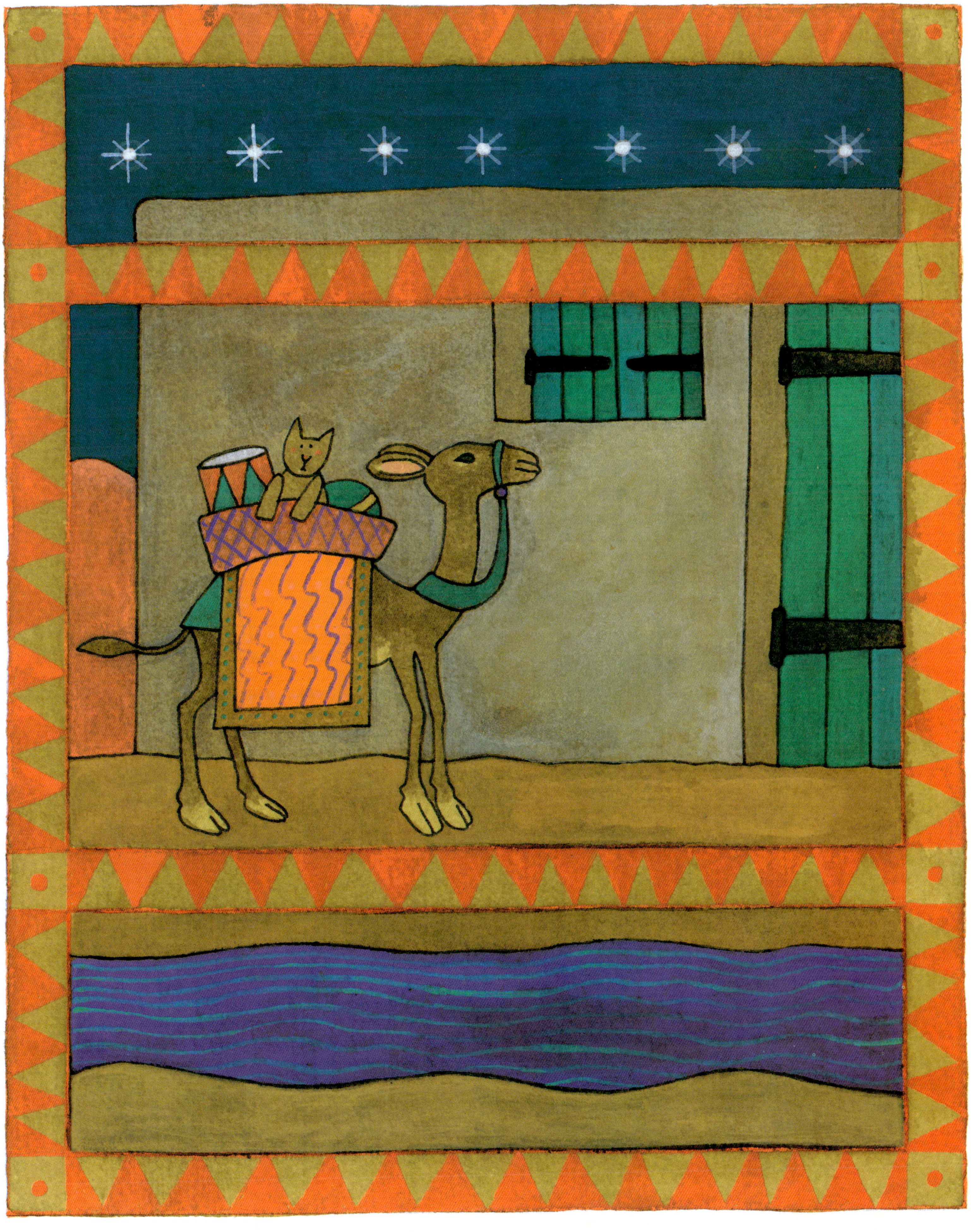

The Legend of the Birds

Squawk! Chirp! Screech!

The birds in the field are always arguing. But on the very first Christmas, they put aside their quarrels, all to help the little Baby Jesus. This is how it happened:

The raven, black as night, was flying across the winter fields near Bethlehem, looking for a late night snack, when suddenly he felt a strange wind on his top feathers. He turned his black head upward and saw a host of white-robed angels flying above him. They made him quite giddy. The wind he felt was from the flapping of their great wings. And though he had seen one or two angels before on his flights, he'd never seen such a crowd of them, a veritable host of angels, and so close.

"What is it?" he croaked. Voice had never been his strong point. In fact he had always been jealous of the songbirds. "Why are you here in such numbers?"

"Good tidings we bring," the angels carolled.

Their voices reminded the raven of songbirds and he felt a pang.

"Good tidings of a babe in a manger." And they continued, in their sweet convincing voices, to tell the raven all about Christ's birth. "Now you must bring the news to the other birds."

"Me?" croaked the raven, his voice almost sweet with anticipation. "But they will not listen. They never do."

"They will listen," promised the angels, banking left in perfect formation and flying quickly towards the East.

So the raven flew straightway back down to earth and called a most extraordinary convocation of fowl. And much to his surprise, the other birds *did* listen, for the raven's voice had softened just this once with the wonder of the news.

When the raven had finished his recitation, the owl hushed them all by the raising of his mighty wings. "This one eve we must all work together," he said. "Without argument." And he looked so stern with his big round eyes that not one bird dared disagree.

So the little wren wove a blanket of feathers and green leaves and moss for the Child and with great dignity carried it to Bethlehem. For that deed she is called to this day *la poulette de Dieu,* God's little chicken.

The rooster announced the birth at daybreak to the town, crying not *cock-a-doodle-doo*, as is his usual call, but in very correct Latin, *Christus natus est*, which means "Christ is born". As you can imagine, this surprised the local farmers.

The little brown nightingale perched on the manger. She blended so well with the wood of the barn that no one even noticed her until she opened her mouth. Then she sang the sweetest lullaby anyone had ever heard.

The robin shielded the Child from the fierce open hearth fire, thus singeing his poor breast so that ever after it was as bright red as the flames.

And the raven, though his voice was never again sweet, lost all envy from that day, for he had been the first bird to hear of Christ's birth — and from the angels themselves.

—*adapted from French legends*

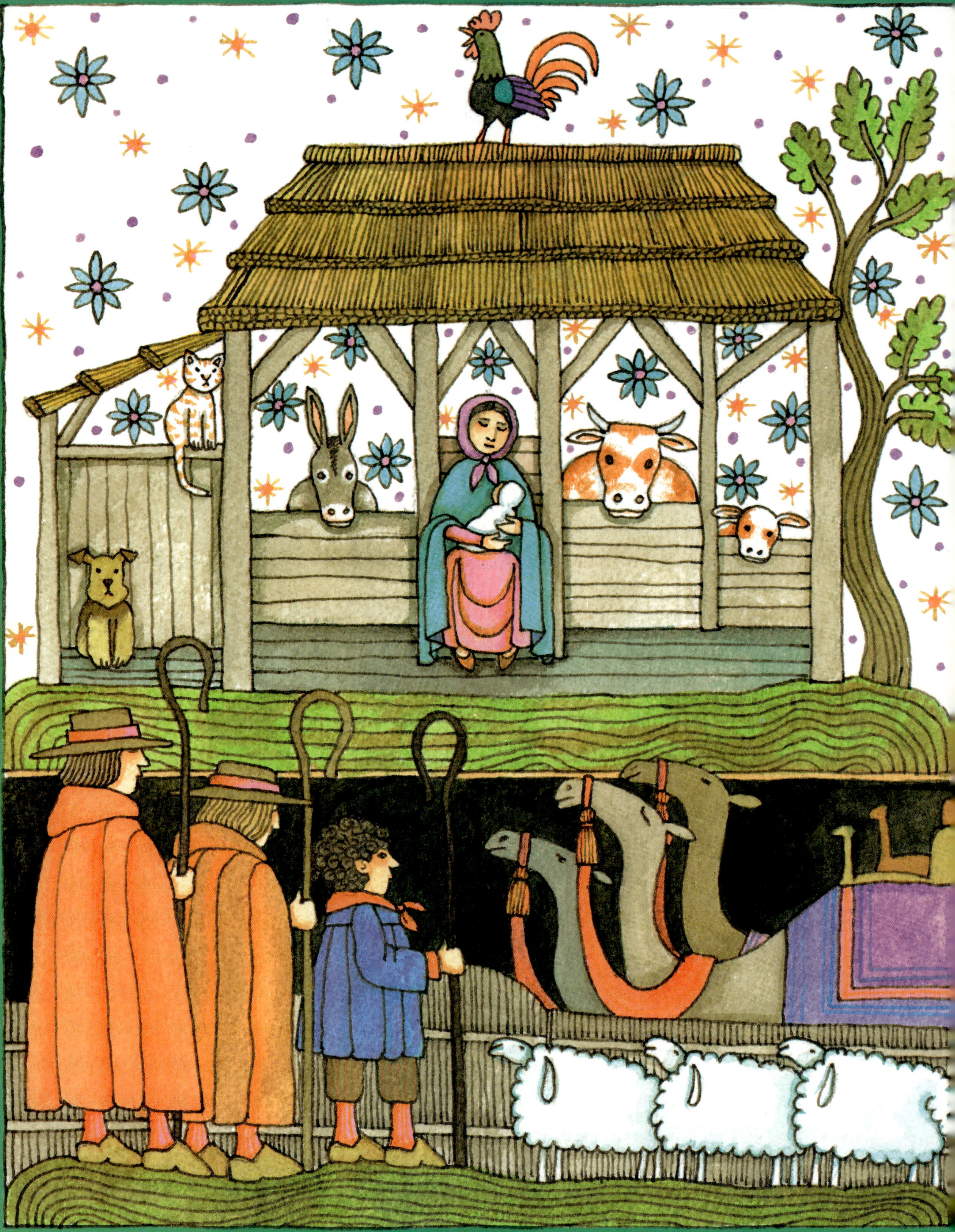

The Stable Hymn

Jane Yolen
Adam Stemple

Steadily

Rooster: 1. — Morning comes and I __ a-wake, And well be-fore the sun I take
A bit of wa-ter for my throat To lu-bri-cate the start-ing note.

Dog: 2. I was as qui-et as __ they bade, And hard-ly an-y sound I made.
I barked at no-one when they came Un-til the Moth-er called __ my name.

Cat: 3. A cat can look up-on __ three kings With all their crowns and cloaks and rings.
And cats can look with stead-y gaze At shep-herds wait-ing all __ a-mazed.

Donkey: 4. I bore a Moth-er wea-ry and worn, I bore her tired and so for-lorn.
I bore her through the wind and rain, And I would bear her o-ver a-gain.

Cow: 5. My own babe lies down at __ my feet, So well do I this vig-il keep.
He is so sleek, I lick his head, And lat-er on he will __ be fed.

Camels: 6. From Ar-a-by, be-neath __ a star, We trav-elled fast, we trav-elled far.
We left the com-fort of our own To find a rude, im-pov-er-ished home.

Shepherds: 7. What cared poor shep-herds for __ these kings, For an-gel songs and an-gel wings?
What cared we frank-in-cense and myrrh? We scarce-ly knew what those things were.

This song must be a gentle tune. My strident wake-up call must croon
And then I stood and viewed the child, A Master who was meek and mild.
And cats can stare down angel choirs Winged and robed and framed in fires.
I bore her past the crowded inn Where no one dared to let her in.
On wholesome milk I give with ease, The palate of my calf I please.
Where are our 'customed silks and gold? And where the wealth the star foretold?
What cared we for hosannas bold, And summer in that winter cold?

To that small burden gently laid Upon the lap of lily maid.
He cannot run or jump or play, Still I'll be faithful from this day.
But ev-'ry cat must drop its eyes Before the One in child disguise.
I bore her to a stable low Where only sheep and oxen go.
But further I shall please the babe That on His Mother's knee is laid.
And where the sceptre? Where the throne? This King, it seems, is all unknown.
What we care for is that dear babe All on His Mother's lap new laid.

For see the babe on Mary's knee. I now must wake Eternity.
Oh, see the babe on Mary's knee, And I am His Eternally.
Oh, see the babe on Mary's knee, I purr before Eternity.
Oh, see the babe on Mary's knee. As I bore her, so I bore He.
Oh, joyous child on Mary's knee, And joy, to feed Eternity.
But, oh, that babe on Mary's knee Is rich as all Eternity.
We sing not for Eternity, But to the child on Mary's knee.

The Donkey's Song

I was cradle and crib
Before the manger.
I was guardian and guard
Against all danger.
I was rocker and rock,
I was God's own cart,
I was breath against cold,
I was His strong heart.

Christmas Plants

What are chilblains?

A nasty swelling brought on by too much cold.

I've got one on my wing. It itches and it hurts. Can you rub some Yule log ashes on it? Merci.

Not too much or she'll have apples growing there instead of feathers!

The Yule Log: Once upon a time, in the cold northern countries of Sweden and Norway, the Norse people believed in *Yggdrasil,* the World Tree. It was said that Yggdrasil had one root in heaven, one root in hell, and one root on earth.

When the Norse became Christians, they burned a log each Christmas to remind themselves that the World Tree had been burned away and with it all their old beliefs.

The custom of burning a special log at Christmas spread all across Europe and into Britain as well. Days before Christmas, families would go into the woods to cut down a large tree. Then, with much singing and laughter, they dragged the great log home on Christmas Eve. Sometimes the log was so big, it took a team of horses to haul it.

Strange customs grew up around the Yule log. For example, some people believed it was unlucky to let the log be burned up completely, so they always saved a little piece for starting the next year's fire.

In France, ashes from the burned log were thought to help heal chilblains. In the Balkans, the ashes were set in the cleft of fruit trees to help bring about a good crop. In Germany, whenever thunder rattled overhead, a piece of the log was put back in the fireplace to help protect the house from lightning.

Mistletoe: Long before there was a Christmas, mistletoe was part of winter solstice celebrations. The Druid priests who lived in ancient Britain thought mistletoe a sacred plant because it did not grow with its roots in the ground. Instead, because it is a parasite, it winds about a tree and roots there. On 22 December each year, the Druid high priest climbed a tall oak and, with a golden sickle, cut down the mistletoe. Underneath the tree, the worshippers caught the pieces with the skirts of their robes. They considered it terribly unlucky to let even the smallest piece touch the ground.

The Norse, too, believed that mistletoe was sacred. Their goddess of love, Frigga, had a son, Balder, who had been killed by an arrow made of mistletoe. When she cried at his death, her tears fell on the mistletoe and turned into white berries. Frigga promised her people that never again would the mistletoe cause harm. She vowed that anyone standing under the mistletoe would get a kiss. Because of that belief, the Norse ruled that enemies meeting under mistletoe—even by accident—had to put up their weapons and declare a truce for the day.

Today our Christmas celebrations mirror some of those old pagan customs. Many people still consider it unlucky to drop mistletoe to the ground. And if you stand under mistletoe at Christmastime, you might be kissed!

Christmas Tree: What would Christmas be today without a Christmas tree? Yet early Christmases were celebrated without them. In fact, according to legend, the custom of Christmas trees began only 1200 years ago with Saint Boniface, a missionary who was trying to convert the pagan German tribes. One day he came upon an awful ceremony. The young prince Asulf was about to be sacrificed on the "blood oak" to the god Thor. Saint Boniface chopped down the oak and rescued Prince Asulf. Where the oak tree fell, a young fir tree sprang up in its place. Saint Boniface told the tribesmen that meant that his God, Christ, would replace their god Thor.

In the Middle Ages churches put on special plays called *miracle plays* to help teach people Bible stories. One of the most popular was "Adam and Eve". In that play, a fir tree hung with bright red apples played the "Paradise Tree." The play and the tree were such a hit, churchgoers put up similar trees in their own homes every 24 December, which is also the Feast of Adam and Eve.

Thor was the god of thunder who carried a big hammer.

I bet he was real thor at Saint Boniface!

Very few people in the Middle Ages could read.

So it was a miracle, indeed, that they could remember their lines in the miracle plays.

By the 1600s, Christmas trees were popular all over Europe. They were trimmed with paper roses, gold foil, apples, and sweets.

By 1840 almost every home in Britain had a Christmas tree. This spread of popularity was due to Prince Albert, who came from Germany to marry Queen Victoria and introduced the first Christmas tree to the royal household. Victorian Christmas trees were decorated with candles, glass baubles, sweets and presents.

All over the world trees are decorated in special ways. In Sweden, painted wooden ornaments and straw figures are popular. In Lithuania, straw birdcages and straw stars are hung on the branches. Painted eggshells have long been used in Czechoslovakia. In Germany, people hang glass trinkets. The Norwegians still decorate with gilded nuts and biscuits and a three-pronged candle for the tree top that symbolizes the three wise men. Japanese Christians put tiny fans and paper lanterns on their trees.

O Christmas Tree

Traditional German carol

With stately grace

O Christmas tree, O Christmas tree, For-ev-er green thy bran-ches.

O Christmas tree, O Christmas tree, For-ev-er green thy bran-ches.

Not on-ly green in sum-mer's glow, But green as well in win-ter snow.

O Christmas tree, O Christmas tree, For-ev-er green thy bran-ches.

The Fir Tree

Oh! said the fir, still green with spring,
I don't get this worshipping
Of distant stars and a distant stranger
Wrapped in cloth in a fusty manger.

I can hold the stars each night
With my boughs, a winking light.
The crescent moon sits on my head.
Why not worship me instead?

Still, if you are set on Glory,
Let me be part of this story.
Take my boughs—a sweeter bed
You could not find to rest His head.

And let me stand up in the manger.
All my lights can ward off danger.
Green I stay—and so will He,
Throughout all eternity.

The First Christmas Tree

Martin Luther was a great man and a great speaker who lived in Germany in the sixteenth century. One Christmas Eve he spoke for hours from the pulpit of a church in a nearby town.

When he rode home that night, he was tired from all the speaking. The air was crisp and cold and as he went along the forest lanes, the sky overhead was sprinkled with stars as thick as sugar on a loaf.

Martin Luther stopped his horse and got down. Tall fir trees towered over him, and above them—far above—were those glittering stars.

Martin Luther sighed aloud, startling his horse. An owl flew away on silent wings.

He wished his wife and children were with him then so that they could see the great beauty in the sky. But they were home in their cozy beds. So he got back on his horse and rode the rest of the way home, the sparkling stars through the fir branches filling him with awe and delight.

Just outside Martin Luther's house was a small cluster of fir trees. After he had stabled his horse, he cut down one little fir and dragged it into the house. He built a wooden stand for it and set it up in front of the great hearth. Last of all he fastened candles to the branches and lit the wicks.

"Come and see, come and see," he called, waking his wife and children. Sleepy-eyed and yawning, they came into the room just as Christmas morning dawned. "Just so, the stars shone down on our Lord through the trees around Bethlehem all those many years ago," he said.

And *that* was the very first Christmas tree.

—*adapted from a German legend*

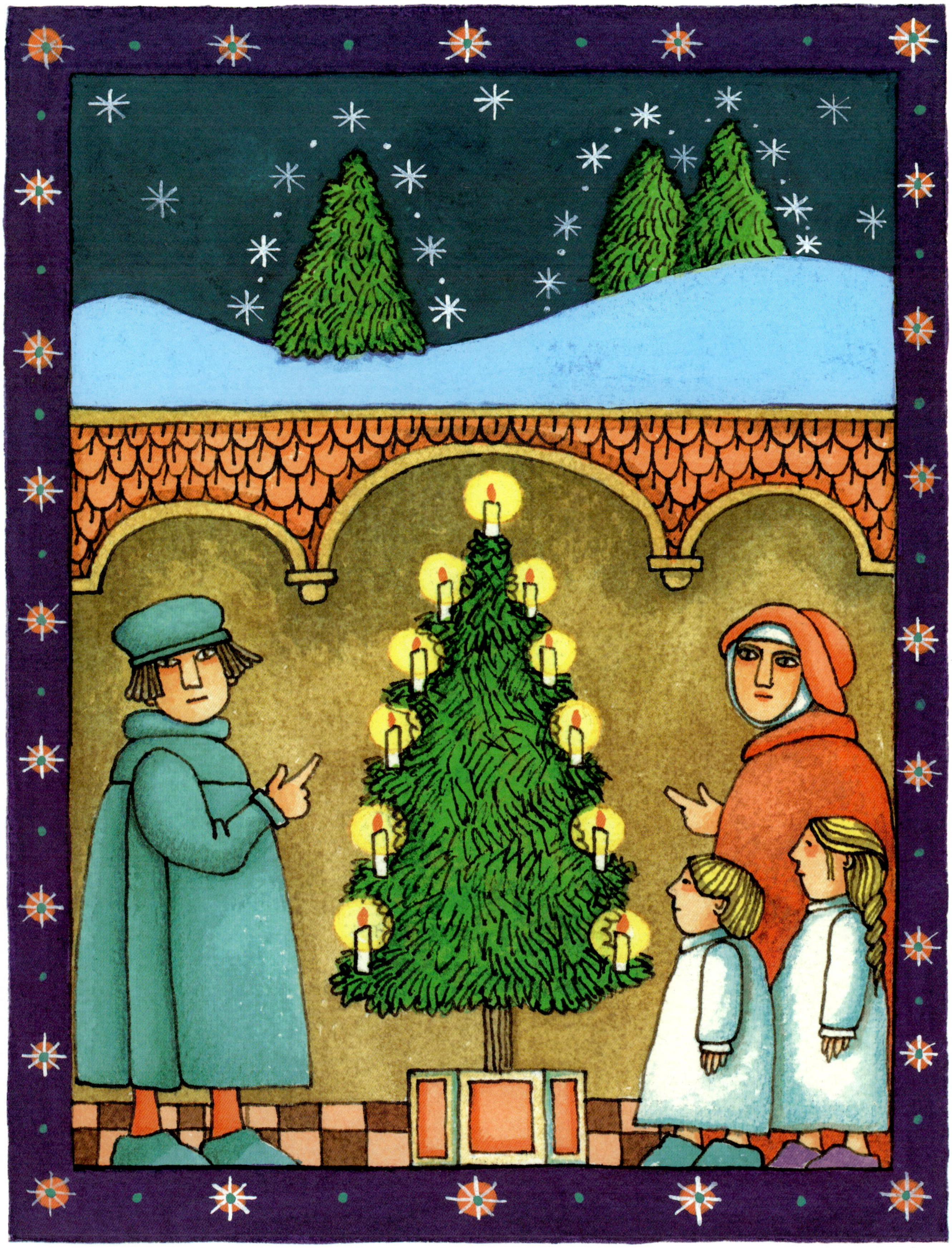

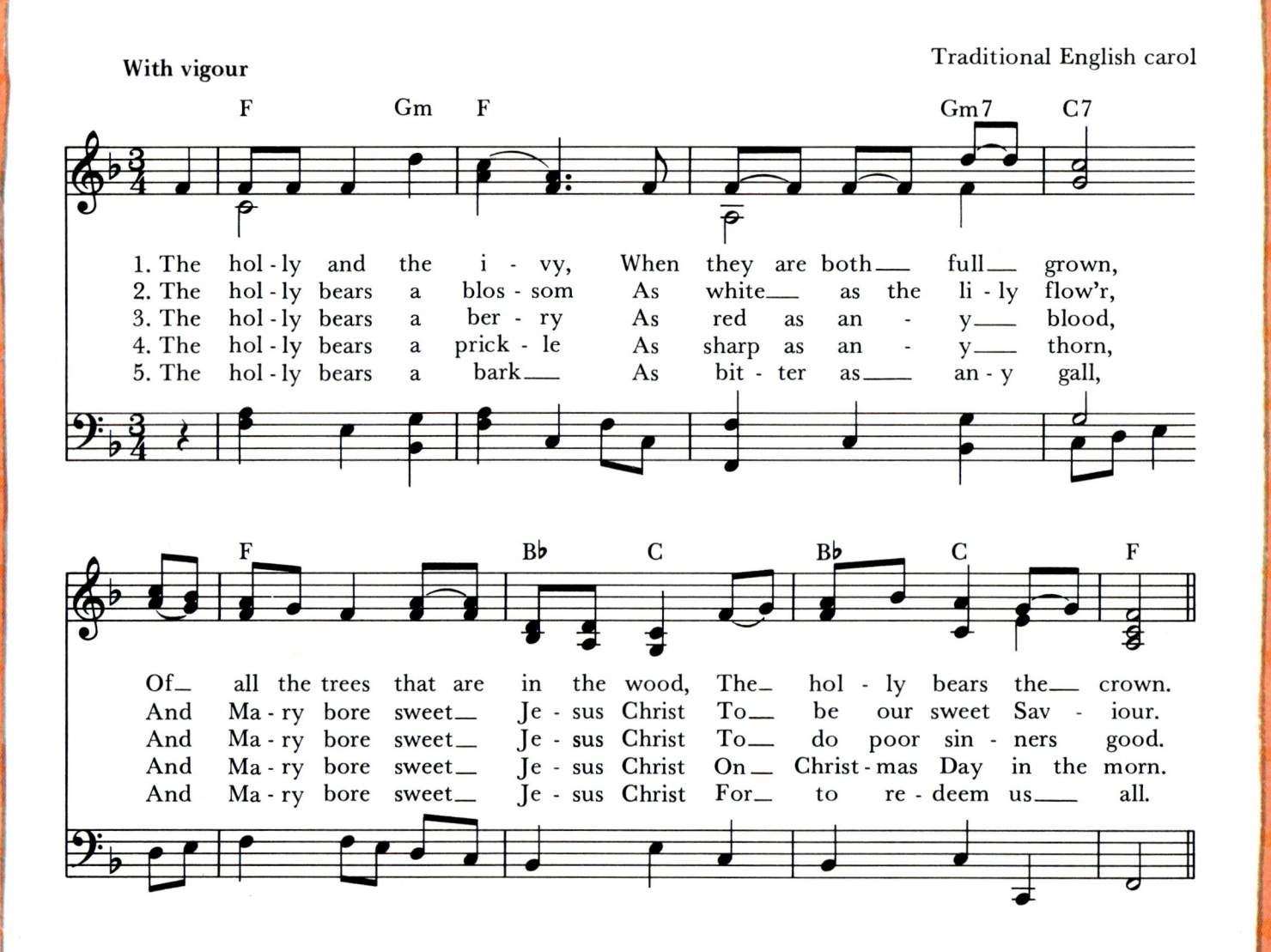

The Holly and the Ivy

With vigour

Traditional English carol

1. The holly and the ivy, When they are both full grown,
2. The holly bears a blossom As white as the lily flow'r,
3. The holly bears a berry As red as any blood,
4. The holly bears a prickle As sharp as any thorn,
5. The holly bears a bark As bitter as any gall,

Of all the trees that are in the wood, The holly bears the crown.
And Mary bore sweet Jesus Christ To be our sweet Saviour.
And Mary bore sweet Jesus Christ To do poor sinners good.
And Mary bore sweet Jesus Christ On Christmas Day in the morn.
And Mary bore sweet Jesus Christ For to redeem us all.

The rising of the sun ___ And the running of the deer, The playing of the merry organ, Sweet singing in the choir.

The Spider's Christmas Tree

One Christmas morning, before the children of the house were awake, a mother spider and her babies discovered the family tree.

Up and down, round and round they crept, looking at the green boughs and the colourful hanging ornaments.

When the Christ Child came into the house to bless the tree, He was dismayed to see grey cobwebs all over it, left by the spiders. Though He loved little spiders—God's busy creatures—He didn't want to disappoint the children of the house.

So He reached out His tiny hand and touched the bottom-most strand. The web instantly turned to silver.

Then the silver ran from strand to strand, from web to web, like a streaking train, until the entire tree shimmered.

And *that* was the first tinsel.

—*adapted from a Ukrainian folk tale*

Yule Log

Twelve days burning,
Twelve nights turning,
Sings the Yule log.

Twelve days warming,
Twelve nights forming,
Sings the Yule log.

Twelve days ashes,
The world watches,
Sings the Yule log.

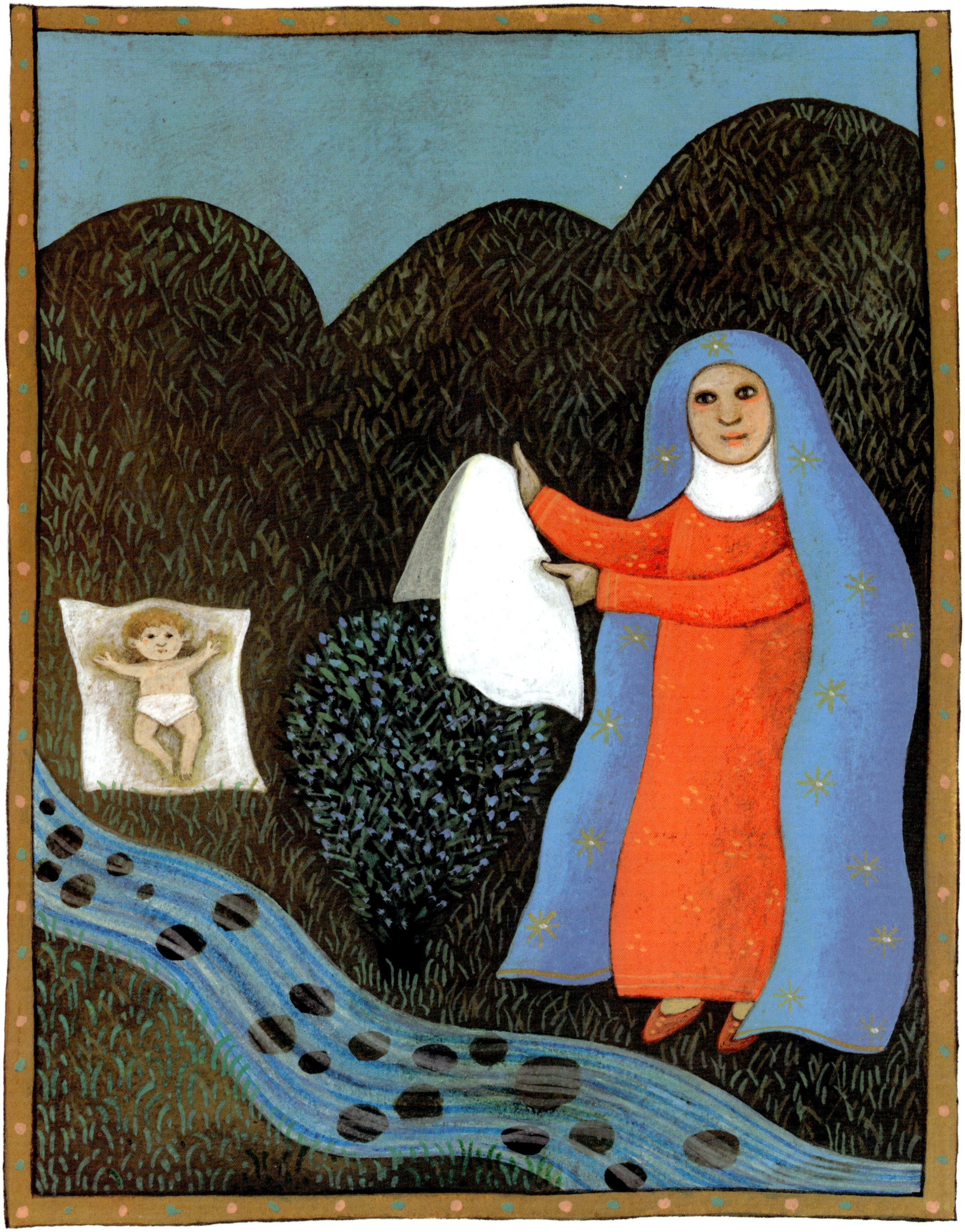

The Legend of Rosemary

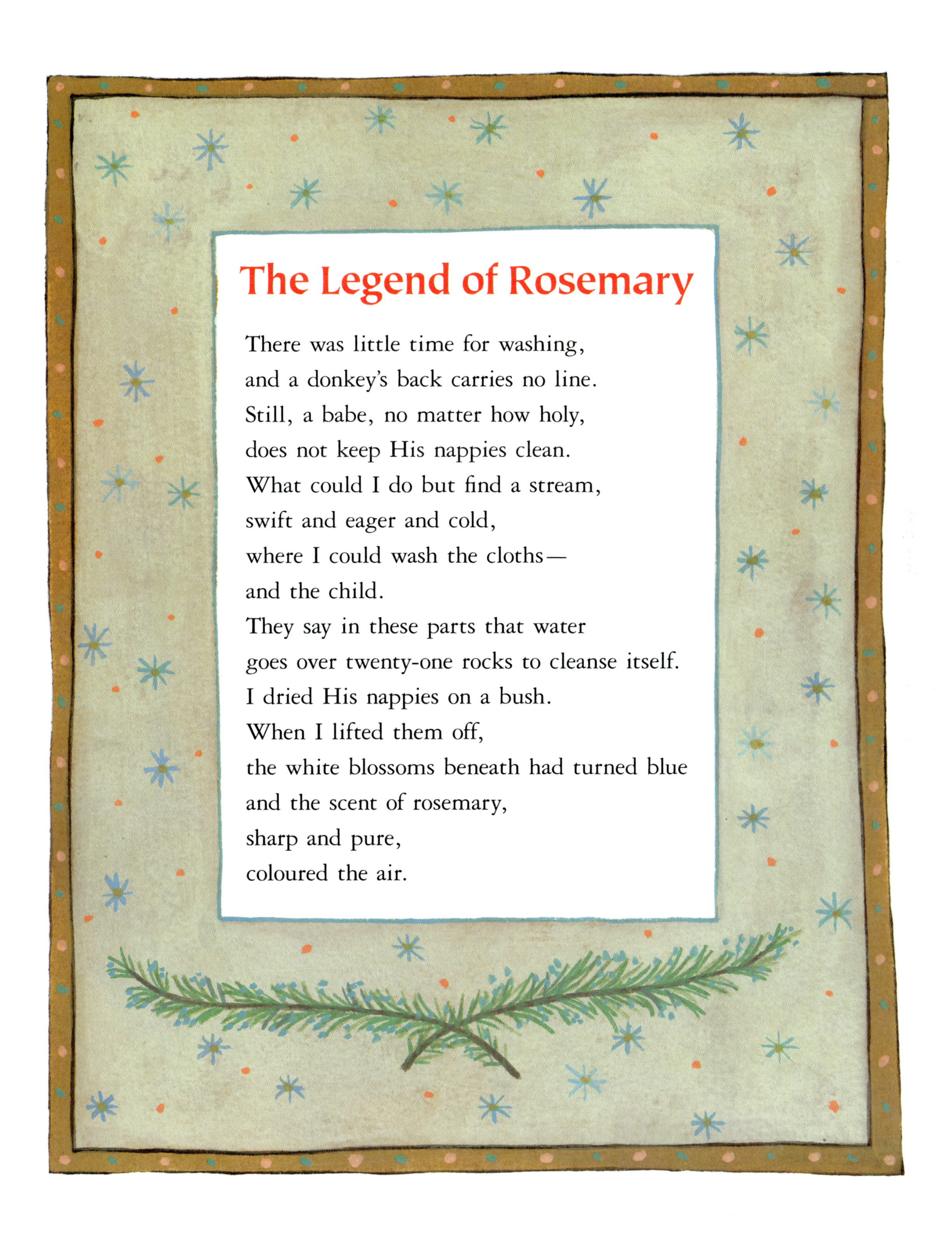

There was little time for washing,
and a donkey's back carries no line.
Still, a babe, no matter how holy,
does not keep His nappies clean.
What could I do but find a stream,
swift and eager and cold,
where I could wash the cloths—
and the child.
They say in these parts that water
goes over twenty-one rocks to cleanse itself.
I dried His nappies on a bush.
When I lifted them off,
the white blossoms beneath had turned blue
and the scent of rosemary,
sharp and pure,
coloured the air.

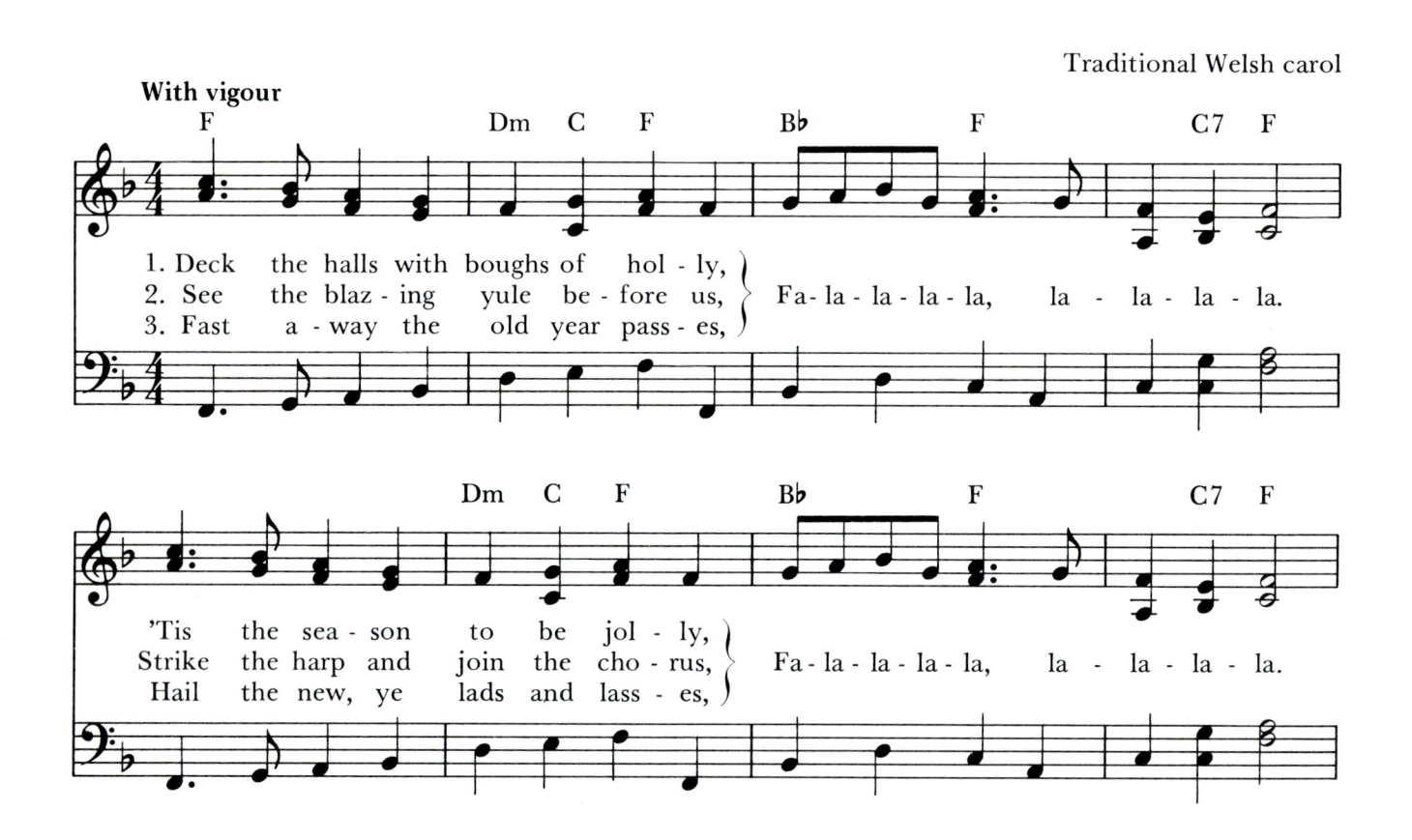

Deck the Halls

Traditional Welsh carol

With vigour

1. Deck the halls with boughs of holly,
2. See the blazing yule before us,
3. Fast away the old year passes,

Fa-la-la-la-la, la-la-la-la.

'Tis the season to be jolly,
Strike the harp and join the chorus,
Hail the new, ye lads and lasses,

Fa-la-la-la-la, la-la-la-la.

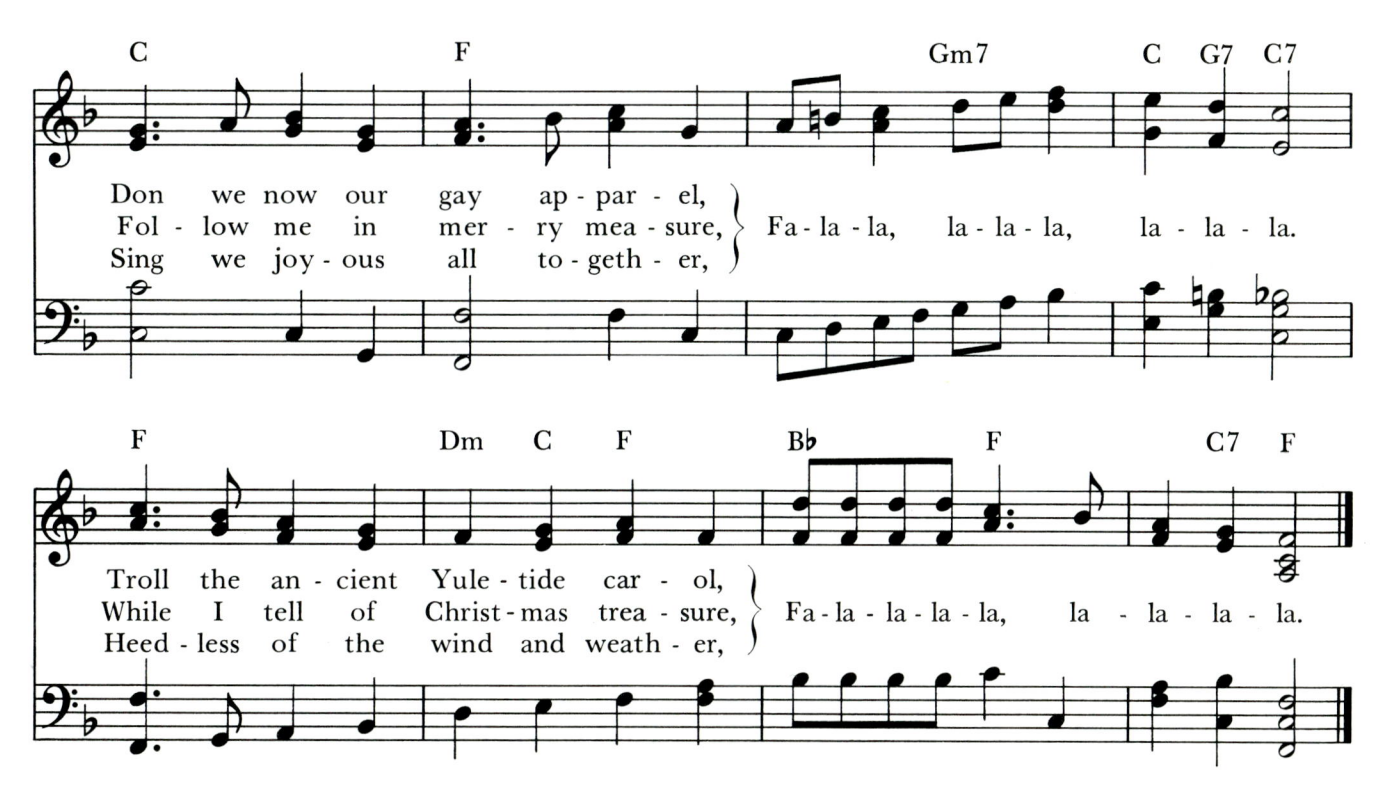

Don we now our gay ap-par-el,
Fol-low me in mer-ry mea-sure, } Fa-la-la, la-la-la, la-la-la.
Sing we joy-ous all to-geth-er,

Troll the an-cient Yule-tide car-ol,
While I tell of Christ-mas trea-sure, } Fa-la-la-la-la, la-la-la-la.
Heed-less of the wind and weath-er,

We Wish You a Merry Christmas

Traditional English carol

With good cheer

1. We wish you a mer-ry Christ-mas, We wish you a mer-ry Christ-mas,
2. Please bring us some fig-gy pud-ding, Please bring us some fig-gy pud-ding,
3. We won't go un-til we get some, We won't go un-til we get some,

We wish you a mer-ry Christ-mas And a hap-py New Year.
Please bring us some fig-gy pud-ding And a cup of good cheer.
We won't go un-til we get some So___ bring it right here!

Chorus

Glad ti-dings we bring to you and your kin,

Glad ti-dings for Christ-mas and a hap-py New Year.

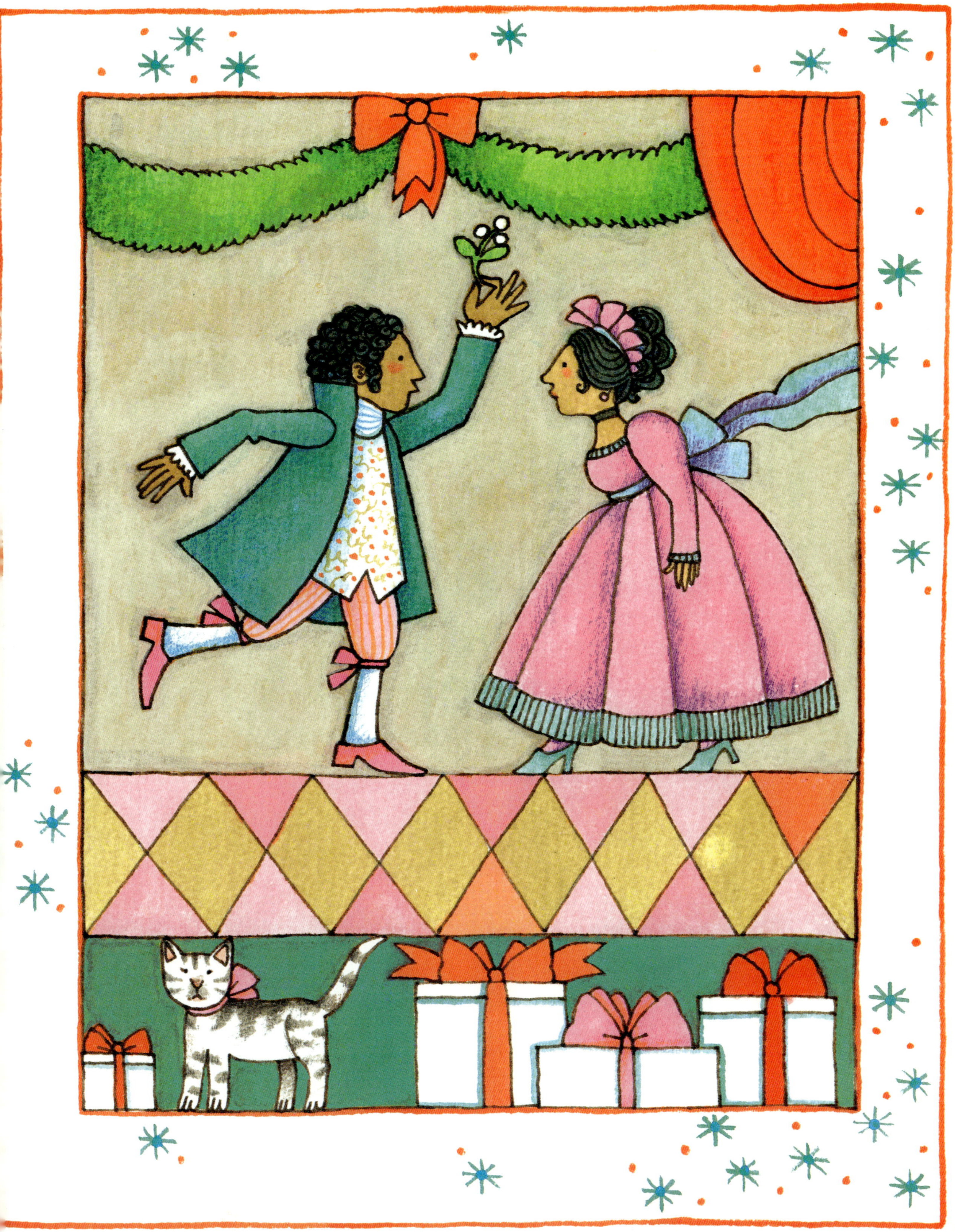

The Dough and the Child

It is said that in the weeks after the birth of Jesus, when Herod's men searched the land for newborn babes with orders to kill them all, the Holy Family fled from one village to the next. But they were so tired, and their little donkey so near exhaustion, that they finally had to stop at a cottage and knock on the door.

"Come in, come in," came the voice of a woman. "My hands are deep in the dough and I cannot open the door for you."

Joseph tied the little donkey by the gate and followed Mary in.

No sooner had they entered and settled by the fire as the goodwife bid them, than there came a loud banging on the door.

"Open up!" a hoarse voice called. "Open up in the name of Herod the King."

Joseph put his hand to his mouth to stifle a cry. But Mary took the babe from her breast and handed him into the woman's doughy hands.

"Here, you must hide him!" Mary said.

Quickly the goodwife dropped the child into the dough, folding him up in it as if he were filling. Then she went back to kneading and shaping the bread.

The door was flung open and six strong soldiers stomped in. They looked at Joseph, who had his arm around Mary. They looked at the goodwife kneading her bread.

"Where is the child?" one soldier called.

"We know one must be here," said another.

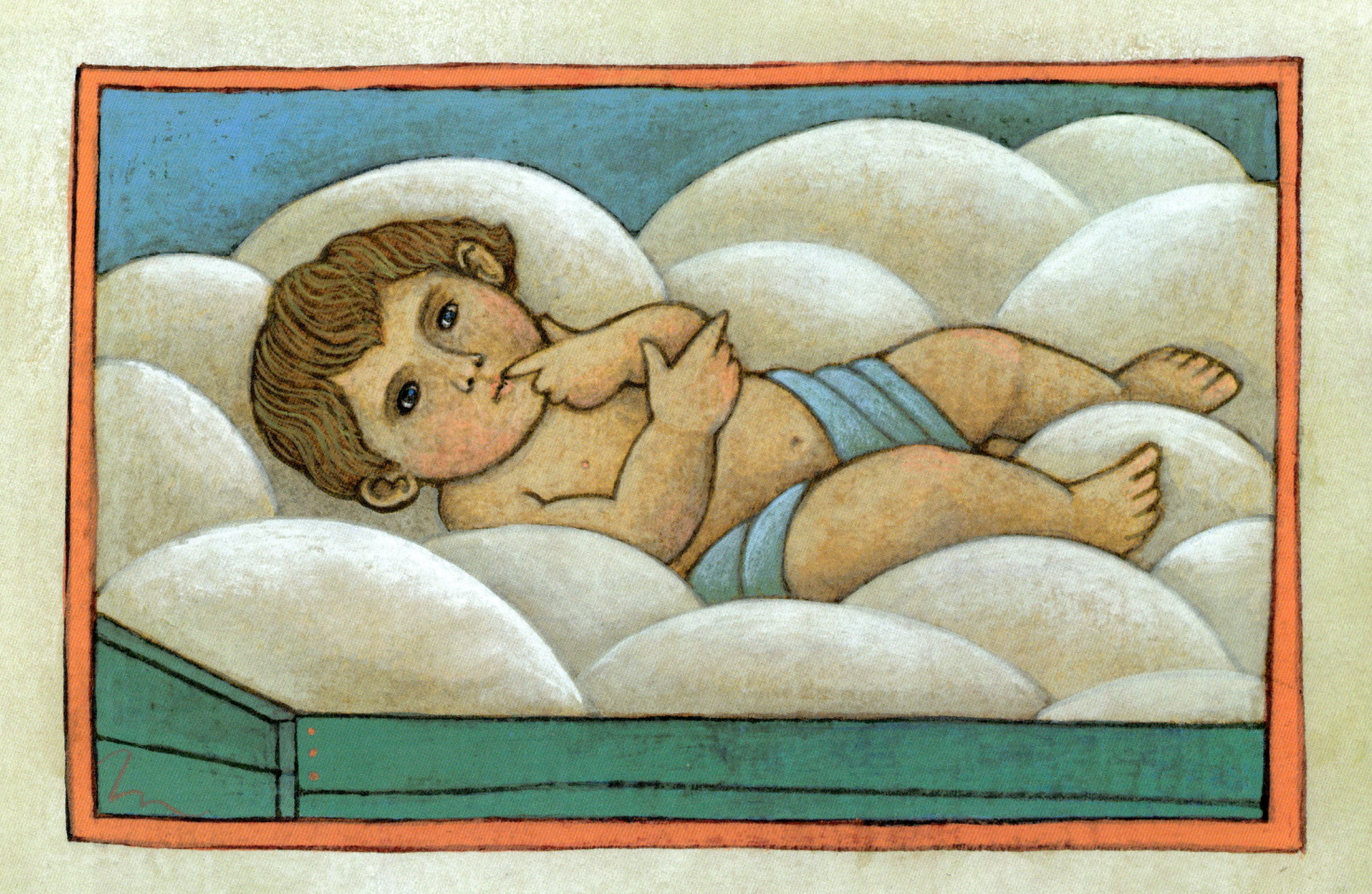

But though they turned the entire house upside down and inside out, they could not find any babe. So at last they went on to the next house, grumbling and slamming the door behind.

As soon as the soldiers were gone, Mary lifted little Jesus from his doughy manger and a strange thing happened. The bread rose higher and higher, as light as any dough could be. And no matter how much of it the goodwife shaped into loaves and put in the oven to bake, there was always some left.

Long after Mary and Joseph and the Baby Jesus went on their way, the goodwife pulled pieces of dough for folk from far and near. And to this very day, small portions of that dough are being saved for the next rising.

—adapted from a medieval legend

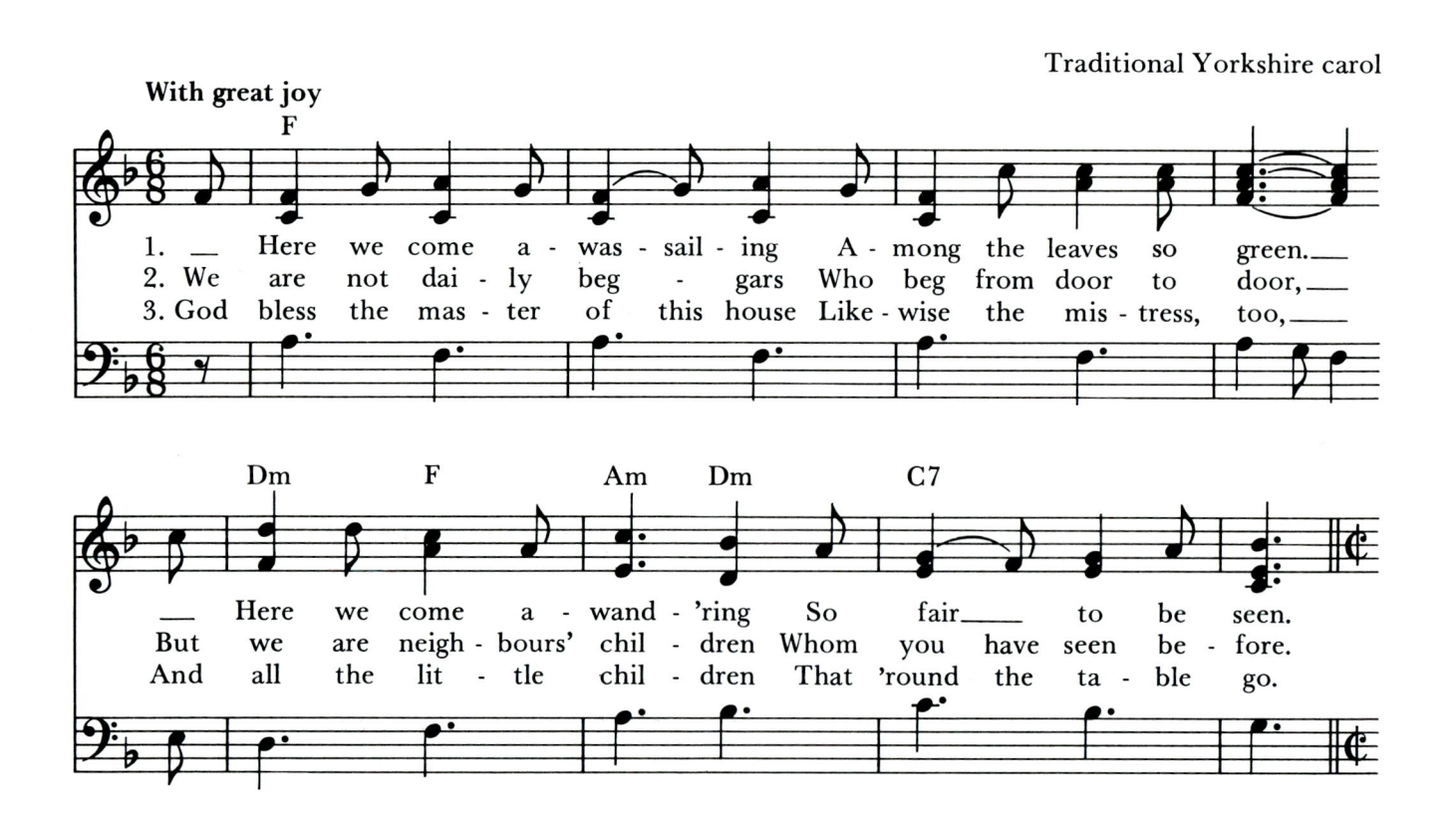

Here We Come A-Wassailing

Traditional Yorkshire carol

With great joy

1. Here we come a-was-sail-ing A-mong the leaves so green.
2. We are not dai-ly beg-gars Who beg from door to door,
3. God bless the mas-ter of this house Like-wise the mis-tress, too,

Here we come a-wand-'ring So fair to be seen.
But we are neigh-bours' chil-dren Whom you have seen be-fore.
And all the lit-tle chil-dren That 'round the ta-ble go.

Chorus

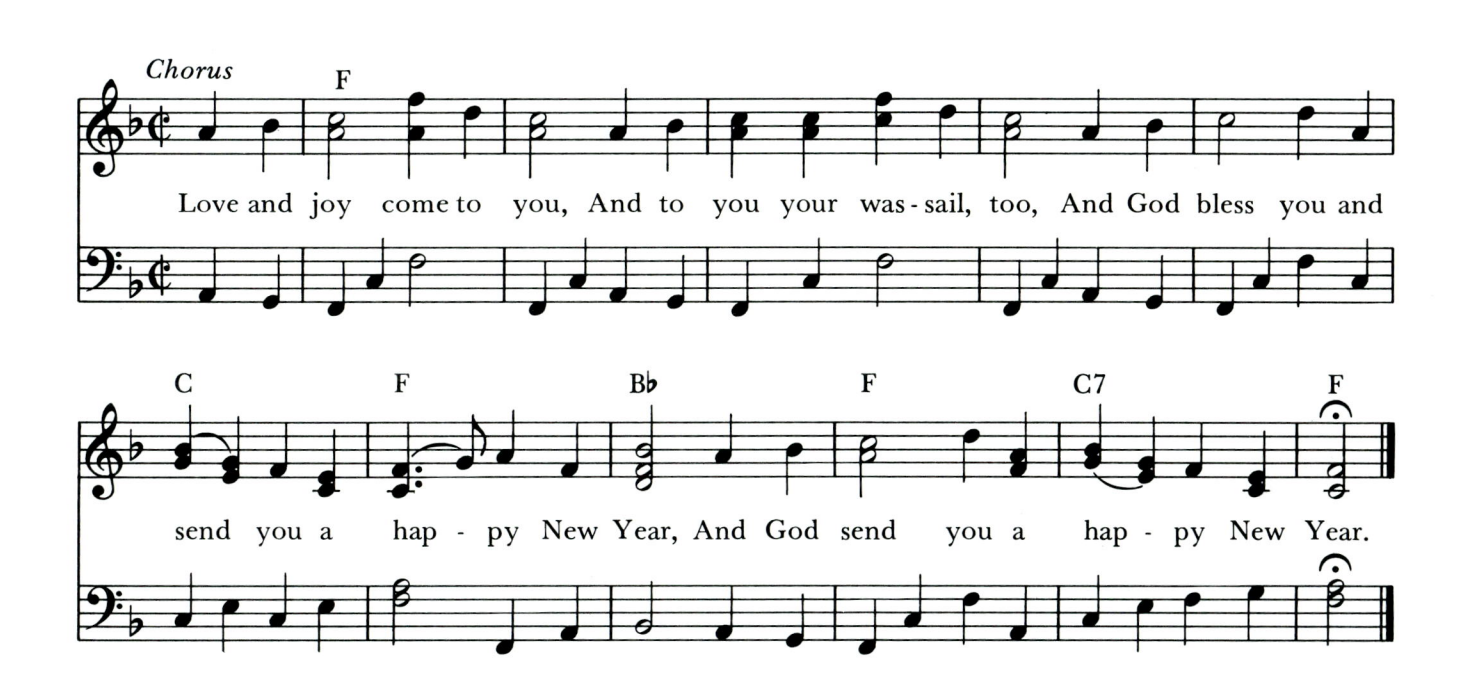

Love and joy come to you, And to you your was-sail, too, And God bless you and send you a happy New Year, And God send you a happy New Year.

The Paignton Christmas Pudding

We will always remember that terrible year
When we planned out our monstrous Pud.
    For the recipe called for a hundred pounds suet,
    An equal proportion of raisins into it,
    And four hundredweights of whole flour to do it,
And many more eggs to the good.

We will always remember that terrible year
With the Pudding three days on the boil.
    It was nine hundred pounds, which could feed half the village,
    And all of the dogs fighting over the spillage,
    The rest of the waste we composted for tillage.
We hoped for good luck with our toil.

We will always remember that terrible year
When the Pudding was brought to the Green.
    It was drawn by three horses—a bay, brown, and black.
    They brought it so far they could not bring it back.
    And there wasn't a thing that our Pudding did lack.
We were sure it was fit for the Queen.

We will always remember that terrible year.
We'd a man on the drum, fife, and fiddle,
    The children, with flags, were let out at half noon,
    And the village housewives each a-banging a spoon,
    And the Morris men dancing a bell-ringing tune.
But that blamed Pud *not done in the middle!*

The Boar's Head Carol

Traditional English
Wynkyn De Worde

With stately grace

1. The boar's head in__ hand bear I, Be-decked with bays and rose-mar-y,
2. The boar's head, as I un-der-stand, Is the fin-est dish in all the land.

And I pray you, my mas-ters, be mer-ry, *Quot est-is in con vi-vi-o.*
Which__ thus be-decked with a gay gar-land, Let us *ser-vi-re can - ti-co.*

Chorus

Ca - put a - pri de - fe - ro, Red - dens lau - des Do - mi - no.

Twelve Pies

Oh sing a song of good luck pies
From Christmas to Epiphany,
And each filled with a sweet surprise.
Oh baker, will you give any?

Some stuffed with meat, some stuffed with mince,
From Christmas to Epiphany,
I haven't had a good pie since.
Oh baker, will you give any?

For one a day we eat our fill
From Christmas to Epiphany,
They bring good luck and right good will.
Oh baker, will you give any?

Christmas Carols

Singing has always been a part of the Christmas story. The angels sang their message of joy to the shepherds in the fields:

> *Gloria in excelsis Deo.*
> Glory to God in the highest,
> and peace on earth,
> good will towards men.

But the first carols were not Christmas songs at all. They were dance tunes, as popular as any songs we dance to today. The word *carol* goes back to the ancient Greek word *choraulein*, meaning a ring dance accompanied by flutes. These original carols were danced by a chain of men and women holding hands and moving while the stanza was sung. Then they stood, marking time with their feet, while singing the chorus.

Everyone loved singing and dancing to carols so much that the church officials finally decided it would be a good idea to make carols a part of the Christmas festivities. Some songs, like "The Holly and the Ivy", are very old pagan tunes with Christian verses added. Others, like "We Three Kings of Orient Are", are more modern.

Although English and German speaking people no longer dance to carols, people in the Latin communities still do. In the great cathedral in Seville, Spain, choir boys move to the music and play castanets as they sing. In Puerto Rico, dance-songs are still very popular at Christmastime, as they are in many of the Central and South American countries.

All over the world there are different Christmas carol customs.

In Italy, on 6 January—Twelfth Night—noisy instruments accompany the songs. In the city of Naples, bagpipers come down from the Abruzzi Mountains and go from house to house playing loud tunes.

In Sweden, children and their parents join hands to sing and dance around the Christmas tree.

In Poland, the carols are called *kolendy* and are sung in a walk around the tree.

In Mexico, children and grownups go in a procession from house to house, asking in song permission to enter. At first they are always refused. But when they explain that it is Mary and Joseph who want to come, they are admitted. The celebration is called *Posada*, which means *inn*.

In the mountain villages of the Austrian Alps, *Anglöckler* or bell ringers go from house to house singing carols (but not ringing bells) on 6 January. They are given the last of the biscuits left hanging on the Christmas trees.

The old choruses were called "burdens".

Why? Was it a hard tune to carry?

Why are they called bell ringers if they don't ring bells?

Because in pagan times they did ring bells and play noisy horns at the winter solstice festivals to frighten away evil spirits.

Hark! The Herald Angels Sing

Charles Wesley
Felix Mendelssohn-Bartholdy

With joy

1. Hark! the her-ald an-gels sing, "Glo-ry to the new-born King;
2. Christ by high-est heav'n a-dored; Christ, the ev-er-last-ing Lord;
3. Hail, the heav'n-born Prince of Peace! Hail, the Sun of Right-eous-ness!

Peace on earth and mer-cy mild,— God and sin-ners re-con-ciled!"
Come, De-sire of Na-tions, come,— Fix in us Thy hum-ble home.
Light and life to all He brings, Ris'n with heal-ing in His wings.

Joy-ful all ye na-tions rise,— Join the tri-umph of the skies;—
Veiled in flesh the God-head see;— Hail th' In-car-nate De-i-ty,—
Mild He lays His glo-ry by,— Born that man no more may die,—

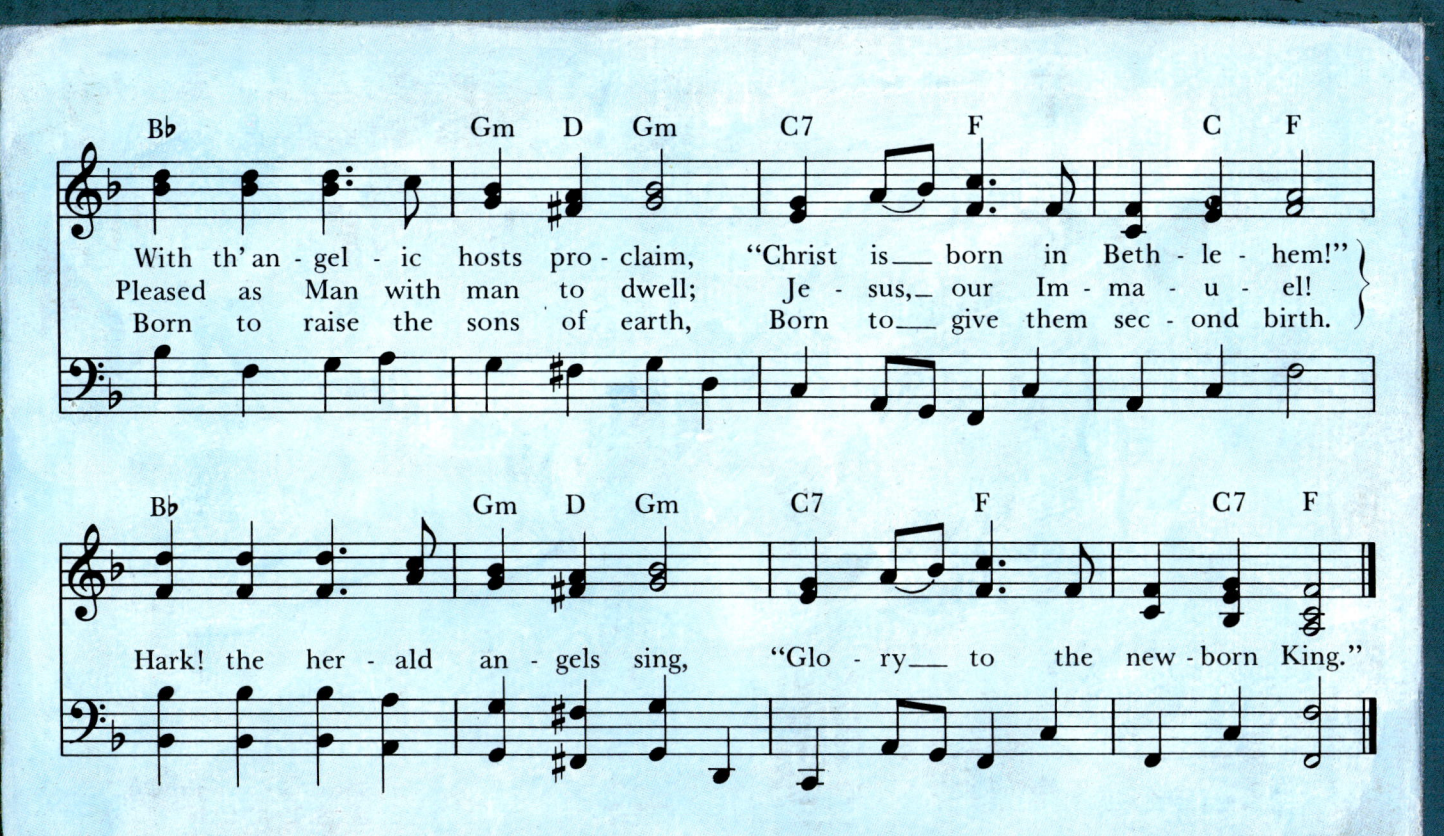

With th' an-gel-ic hosts pro-claim, "Christ is born in Beth-le-hem!"
Pleased as Man with man to dwell; Je-sus, our Im-ma-u-el!
Born to raise the sons of earth, Born to give them sec-ond birth.
Hark! the her-ald an-gels sing, "Glo-ry to the new-born King."

The Foolish Shepherd:
A Play in Verse

Characters:

Piper   Dicer 1   Dicer 2   Sleeper

Singing Chorus   Foolish Shepherd   Angel   Singing Chorus

(The curtains open on a field where four shepherds can be seen. One is playing a pipe, two are playing at dice or bones, one is fast asleep. A fifth shepherd runs in from stage left, waving his crook over his head. His robes flap about his ankles frantically and he calls out in a high-pitched yodel.)

Foolish: Help! Help! Help!
It came at me out of the sky.
It came at me—I thought I'd die.
It came at me, a kind of hawk,
With wings this big. (*He stretches his arms wide.*)
And it could talk.

Piper: Don't be silly. Don't be daft.
Wings that big. (*He winks at other shepherds.*)
I would have laughed!

Dicer 1: It really talked? Now—go away.

Dicer 2: What does a big bird have to say?

Piper: Bwaaaaaak. Bwaaaaaak. (*He flaps his arms madly.*)

Foolish: He sang about a lowly manger
Where the world's hope—and all its danger—
Is to be born this blessed night.

Dicer 1: And then—don't tell me—he took flight!
Bwaaaaak. Bwaaaaak.

Sleeper: (*yawning*) What a dream—a shining star
                Bringing three great kings afar.
                They carried frankincense and myrrh.

Dicer 2:   So, tell us what those frank-things were.

Sleeper: In my dream it all made sense.
                But...(*he shrugs*) the meanings have all flown hence.

Piper: Like *his* wits. (*pointing to Foolish*) And like his bird.
                A hawk that talks. That's so absurd.

Dicer 1:   A bird whose wingspread is so great—
                It's lucky he already ate,
                Or Foolish, here, would be inside
                The bird and going for a ride
                To nest and nestlings. HELLO DINNER!
                I'VE BROUGHT YOU A LIKELY SINNER.

All except Foolish: Yum! (*They rub their bellies.*)

Sleeper: Speaking of sins—he's left the sheep!

Piper: And this time was *his* watch to keep.
Dimwit! (*He swats Foolish.*) Idiot!

Dicer 1:   Loony!

Dicer 2:   Fool!

Sleeper: "Watch sheep first" is our one rule.

(*All swat poor Foolish until he is on his knees.*)

Angel: (*flies in, circles the swatters and Foolish on his knees*)
HARK. Now shepherds, HARK.
(*looks around, whispers to himself*)
Now where is a good place to park?
Flying so far, so fast, is tiring.
My wings are sore—and I'm perspiring.
HARK, I say, good shepherds, HEAR.

Piper: (*looking up and seeing the angel*) I tremble.

Dicer 1: I shiver.

Dicer 2: I faint.

Sleeper: I fear.

Foolish: (*stands, all smiles now*)
There—you see—it said its name,
A Hark—and that was what I claimed.

Sleeper: Hey—it was in my dreaming, too.

Piper: A hawk that big should be in the zoo.
We'll capture it and make the news.
Come on guys—how can we lose?

Dicer 1: I have a net.

Dicer 2: I have a spear.

Piper: You grab its wings...

Angel: Hark, shepherds, hear!

(*Piper, Dicer 1 and 2 capture the angel*)

Sleeper: That's definitely not my dream.
But things are seldom what they seem.
(*He puts his hand on the angel's wing.*)

Angel: (*Singing*) Glory to God in the highest;
And peace on earth,
Good will to men.

Piper: That's just squawking, squeaks, and cries.
Close your ears; it's just bird lies.
What do big birds know of men?
They know the eagle, owl, and wren,
They know the robin, finch, and dove.
They know the turkey, goose, and

Angel: LOVE;
And PEACE and JOY I bring,
And of the King of Kings I sing.

(*All except Foolish cover their ears at what they consider noise, and groan out loud.*)

Foolish: I'll set you free. Look—here's a knife!
 (*He cuts away the net.*)

Angel: I'll teach you of eternal life.
 (*Angel takes Foolish's hand.*)

(*Hand in hand Foolish and Angel fly off stage towards a great light.*)

Dicer 1: There goes our catch.

Dicer 2: There goes our game.

Sleeper: There goes the news and possible fame.

Piper: There goes our Foolish—and I've a hunch
 He's just in time for big bird's lunch.

Dicer 1: I wonder if he's soup or snack.

Dicer 2: Or if that bird is coming back. (*He picks up the spear.*)

Sleeper: Now someone has to guard the sheep.
It's not *my* turn. I need my sleep. (*He lies down.*)

Dicer 1:   Not my turn.

Dicer 2:   Not my turn either.
It's really yours. (*He points at Piper.*)

Piper: It is not neither.
(*He turns and stares offstage after Angel and Foolish.*)
Though I wonder what we've missed tonight.

Sleeper: While you are at it—turn off that light.

Foolish's voice (from offstage): Oh Hark, I'm glad I set you free;
I'm glad for all eternity.

(*From offstage, where the light shines, comes the sound of first angels and then others singing "Hark the Herald Angels Sing" as the light on the stage goes off and the light from offstage shines on and on. Angels march on stage carrying candles and singing; next shepherds; and finally animals, all singing. But not the Piper, Dicers 1 and 2, or Sleeper, who we do not see again.*)

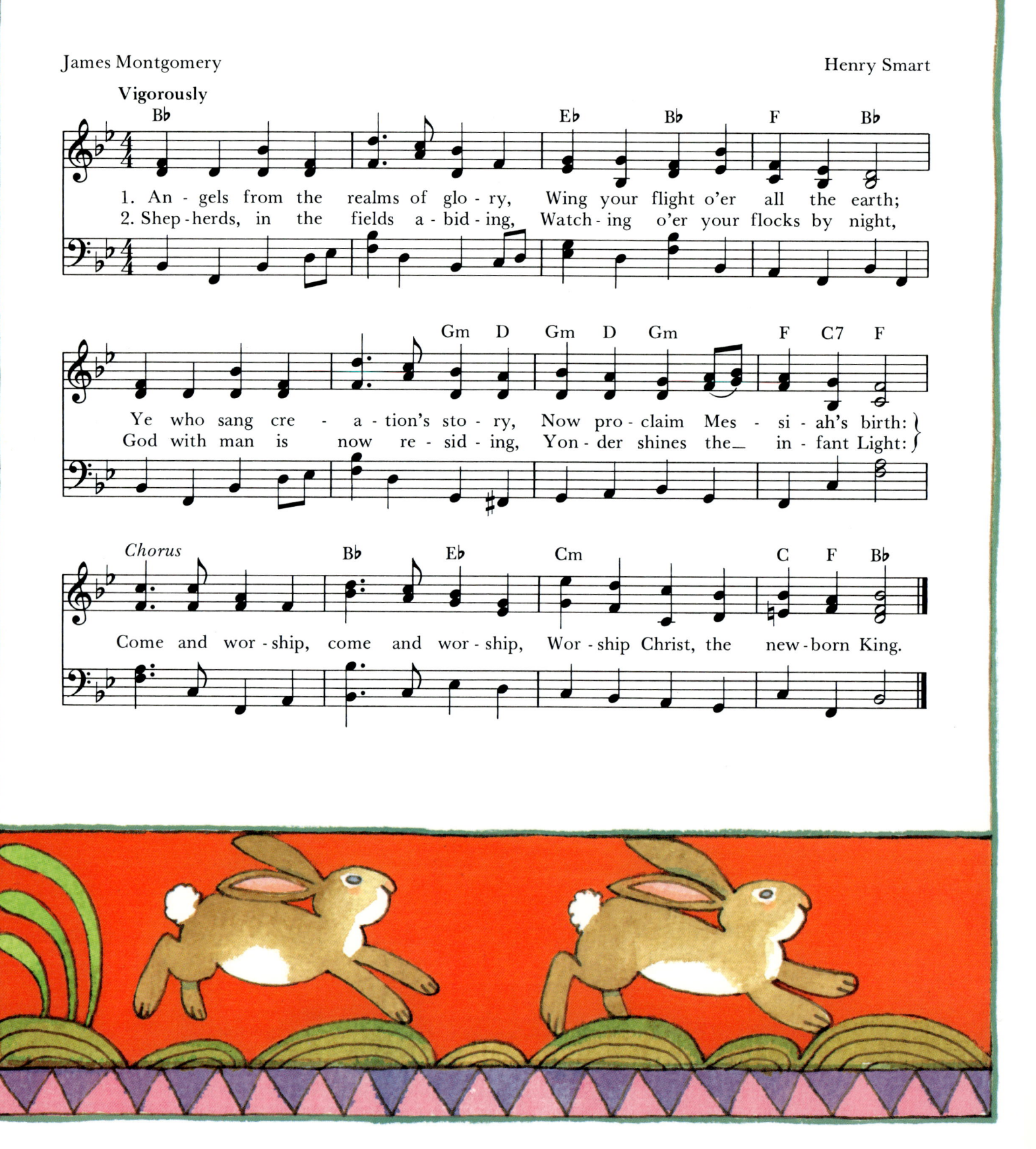

Angels From the Realms of Glory

James Montgomery
Henry Smart

Vigorously

1. An-gels from the realms of glo-ry, Wing your flight o'er all the earth;
2. Shep-herds, in the fields a-bid-ing, Watch-ing o'er your flocks by night,

Ye who sang cre - a-tion's sto-ry, Now pro-claim Mes - si - ah's birth:
God with man is now re - sid-ing, Yon-der shines the in-fant Light:

Chorus

Come and wor-ship, come and wor-ship, Wor-ship Christ, the new-born King.

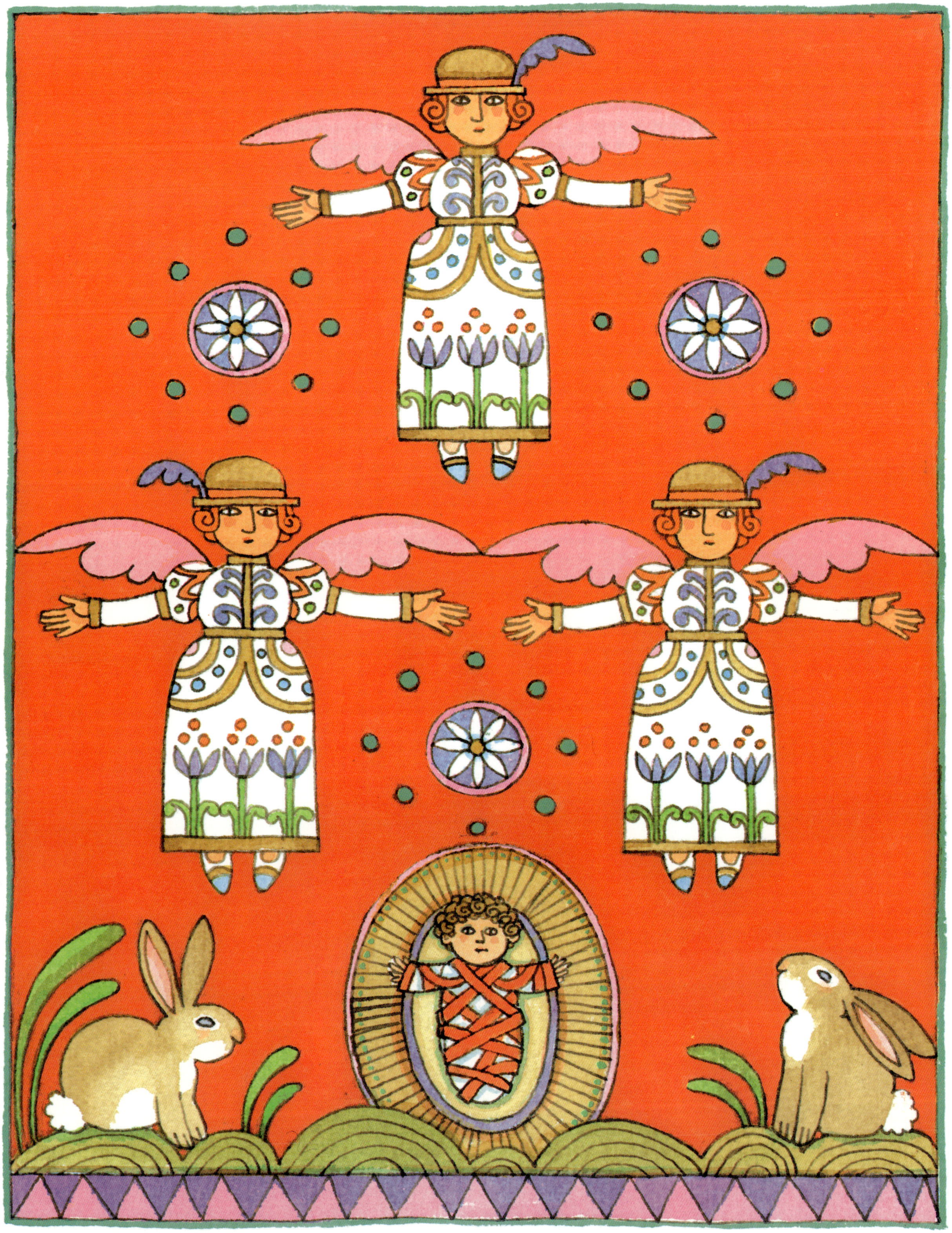

Singing Carols

The night is crisp and very cold
And moonshine lights our way
As we go house to house and sing
About that special day.

And Heidi's voice comes straining through
The scarf that Mama knit,
And Adam's boots are much too big
And only sort of fit.

And Jason's lost a mitten back
By Mrs Rankin's walk,
So with his fingers in his mouth
He finds it hard to talk.

Then Heidi's voice goes very loud,
And Adam's voice is low,
And Jason never hits a note
That any of us know.

But at each house we sing some songs,
Like "Deck the Halls" and such.
The neighbours smile and call our names
Perhaps that isn't much—

But it was not so different when
Two thousand years ago
The angels singing brought big smiles
To shepherds in the snow.

Angel Tunes

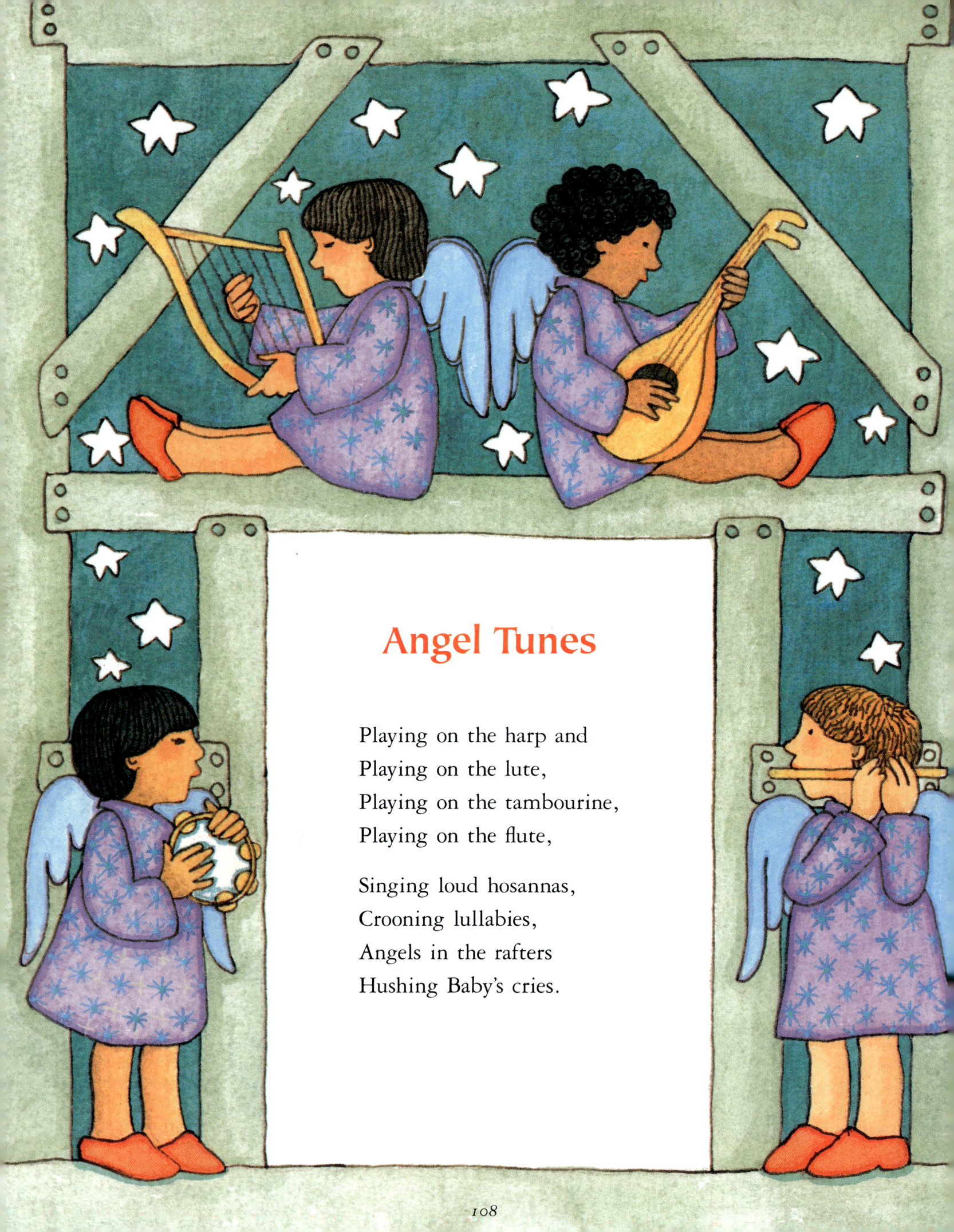

Playing on the harp and
Playing on the lute,
Playing on the tambourine,
Playing on the flute,

Singing loud hosannas,
Crooning lullabies,
Angels in the rafters
Hushing Baby's cries.

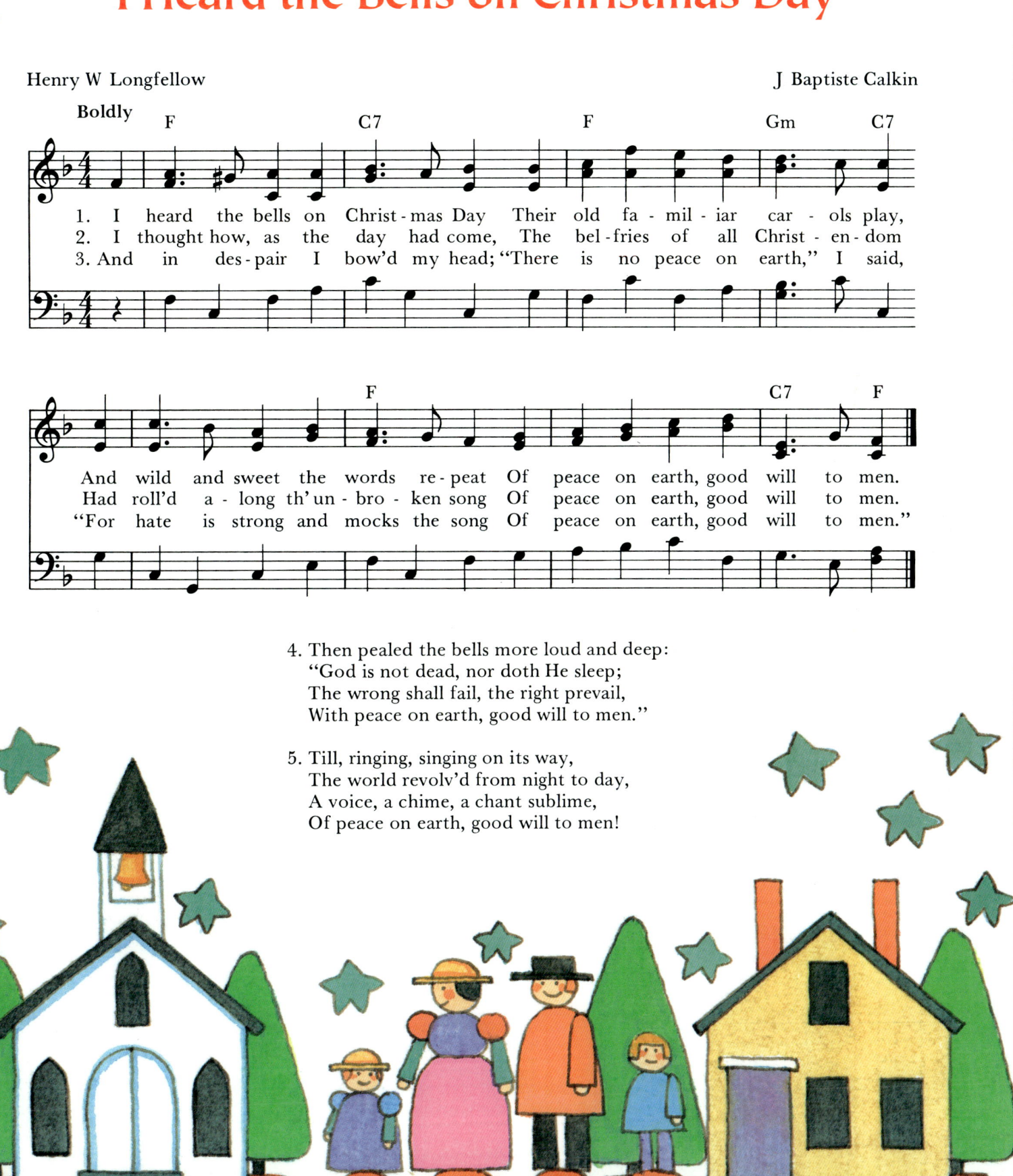

I Heard the Bells on Christmas Day

Henry W Longfellow J Baptiste Calkin

1. I heard the bells on Christ-mas Day Their old fa-mil-iar car-ols play,
2. I thought how, as the day had come, The bel-fries of all Christ-en-dom
3. And in des-pair I bow'd my head; "There is no peace on earth," I said,

And wild and sweet the words re-peat Of peace on earth, good will to men.
Had roll'd a-long th'un-bro-ken song Of peace on earth, good will to men.
"For hate is strong and mocks the song Of peace on earth, good will to men."

4. Then pealed the bells more loud and deep:
   "God is not dead, nor doth He sleep;
   The wrong shall fail, the right prevail,
   With peace on earth, good will to men."

5. Till, ringing, singing on its way,
   The world revolv'd from night to day,
   A voice, a chime, a chant sublime,
   Of peace on earth, good will to men!

Santa Claus and Giving Gifts

Santa Claus as we know him today is only two hundred years old. But long before our Santa Claus, there were Christmas gift bringers. Even before that, presents were exchanged at the winter solstice festivals.

Early gift givers included the Norse god Odin riding his eight-footed horse, Sleipnir, and the German goddess Hertha who brought gifts of good fortune and health. At the Roman Saturnalia the rich gave gifts to the poor and the poor gave garlands of holly and laurel. The Jewish people celebrated Chanukah in the winter with gifts for each of the eight days, and the custom continues today.

The Three Kings (or the Wise Men or the Magi) brought gifts to the Baby Jesus, arriving at the stable on 6 January, or Three Kings' Day, according to tradition. Their presents were gold, the symbol of kingship; frankincense, for the high priesthood; and myrrh, as a sign that Christ would be a healer. Each of the three kings ruled a different country. Old, white-bearded Melchior was king of Nubia and Arabia. Young Kaspar headed Tarsus, a city in Turkey. And Balthasar, the black king, was lord of Ethiopia.

So Odin rode an eight-footed horse.

And the Three Kings rode camels.

How did Santa Claus find reindeer then?

Turned right at the North Pole!

St Nicholas lived in the fourth century and was a bishop in the city of Myra in Asia Minor. He was known for his kindness and his love of children. It was said that he once brought three murdered schoolboys back to life. The most famous story about St Nicholas and his goodness tells how he helped an impoverished merchant who had lost all his money. The merchant's three daughters were to be sold into slavery to pay his debts. Nicholas tossed a bag of gold into the window and so the first girl was saved. He did it again for the second. When he threw in the third bag, the merchant found out and soon the story of Nicholas's generosity was all over the city. After that, anyone receiving an unexpected gift thanked the bishop. He was made a saint in AD 800 by the Eastern Church.

Sinterklas is the Dutch name for St Nicholas. Dutch children believe that he sails over from Spain with his Moorish helper Black Peter, who climbs down chimneys carrying a sack full of presents.

Svaty Miklaus is the Czechoslovakian gift giver who is let down from heaven by means of a golden cord held by angels.

SINTERKLAS · ST. NICHOLAS · SVATY MIKLAUS

Befana is the Italian gift giver, an old woman who was too busy cleaning her house to go with the Wise Men to Bethlehem. According to legend, she searches the world over every Epiphany Eve, leaving gifts and sweets in the shoes of sleeping children just in case one of them is the Child she seeks. The Russian version of Befana is the old woman Baboushka.

Jultomten is a Swedish gnome with a red cap and a long white beard who rides on a sleigh pulled by a goat. He brings presents on Christmas Eve and the children leave out bowls of porridge for him as well as carrots for his goat.

Father Christmas is the gigantic British gift bringer who wears a scarlet robe lined with fur. He is crowned with holly or ivy or mistletoe and takes part in mummers' plays at Christmas.

Cristkindl is the Baby Jesus himself as a gift giver, bringing presents to German children on Christmas Eve. Travelling on a pure white donkey, He leaves "Christ's bundles" of food, caps, mittens, and toys as well as the occasional birch rod as a warning to be good.

CRISTKINDL | BEFANA | FATHER CHRISTMAS | JULTOMTEN

Santa Claus is the American version of the gift giver. He was made popular by two American writers and one political cartoonist.

In the early 1800s, the famous author Washington Irving wrote a number of stories about Dutch settlers in New York City. St Nicholas was a character in several of the tales. He rides over the tops of trees in a horse-drawn wagon, filling Christmas stockings that hang by the fire, and smoking a long Dutch pipe.

Author Clement Moore added more details, some of which he borrowed from other sources, when he wrote his famous poem "A Visit from St. Nicholas". He probably took the reindeer from a children's poem called "The Children's Friend". The trip down the chimney he patterned after the Dutch Black Peter. He may even have known about the Jultomten because he describes St Nicholas as "a right jolly old elf".

Thomas Nast was a well-known political cartoonist who drew many pictures of Santa Claus from 1863 to 1886 in the Christmas issues of the popular American magazine *Harper's Weekly.* Nast invented Santa's workshop, Santa answering letters from boys and girls, and even Santa drawing up lists of good and bad children. Nast was also the first to draw a picture of Santa at the North Pole. His cartoons feature a fat, jolly Santa with a red fur-trimmed jacket and a full white beard, just the way we think of Santa Claus today.

We wish... you... a Merry... Christmas!

The North Pole Express

Jane Yolen Adam Stemple

With drive

1. When I got to the station it was very late at night.
2. Outside the fir trees flashing by were hung with strands of ice.
3. And when my spirits were about as low as they could go,

Ex - cept for the con - duc - tor, not a grown-up was in sight.
And on - ly to a po - lar bear would it be Par - a - dise.
The train gave quite a shud - der and then it be - gan to slow.

F7

I climbed a - board the train and saw that it was fill - ing fast,
My teeth were all a - chat - ter and a - clat - ter were my knees,
From some - where not too far a - way a bell be - gan to ring

C

So I found my - self a red plush seat and set - tled down at last.
And soon e - nough I knew that all my limbs would start to freeze.
And one by one the kids jumped up and all be - gan to sing.

G7

My breath streamed out be-fore me and my thoughts streamed out be-hind.
The din - ing car was o - pen and my stom - ach said, "Let's eat!"
And sud - den - ly I found that I was stand - ing in the aisle

F7

I looked out of the win - dow and I won - dered what we'd find—
I stum - bled for - ward lurch - ing on two ver - y fro - zen feet.
And sing - ing, too, and on my face a hap - py Christ - mas smile.

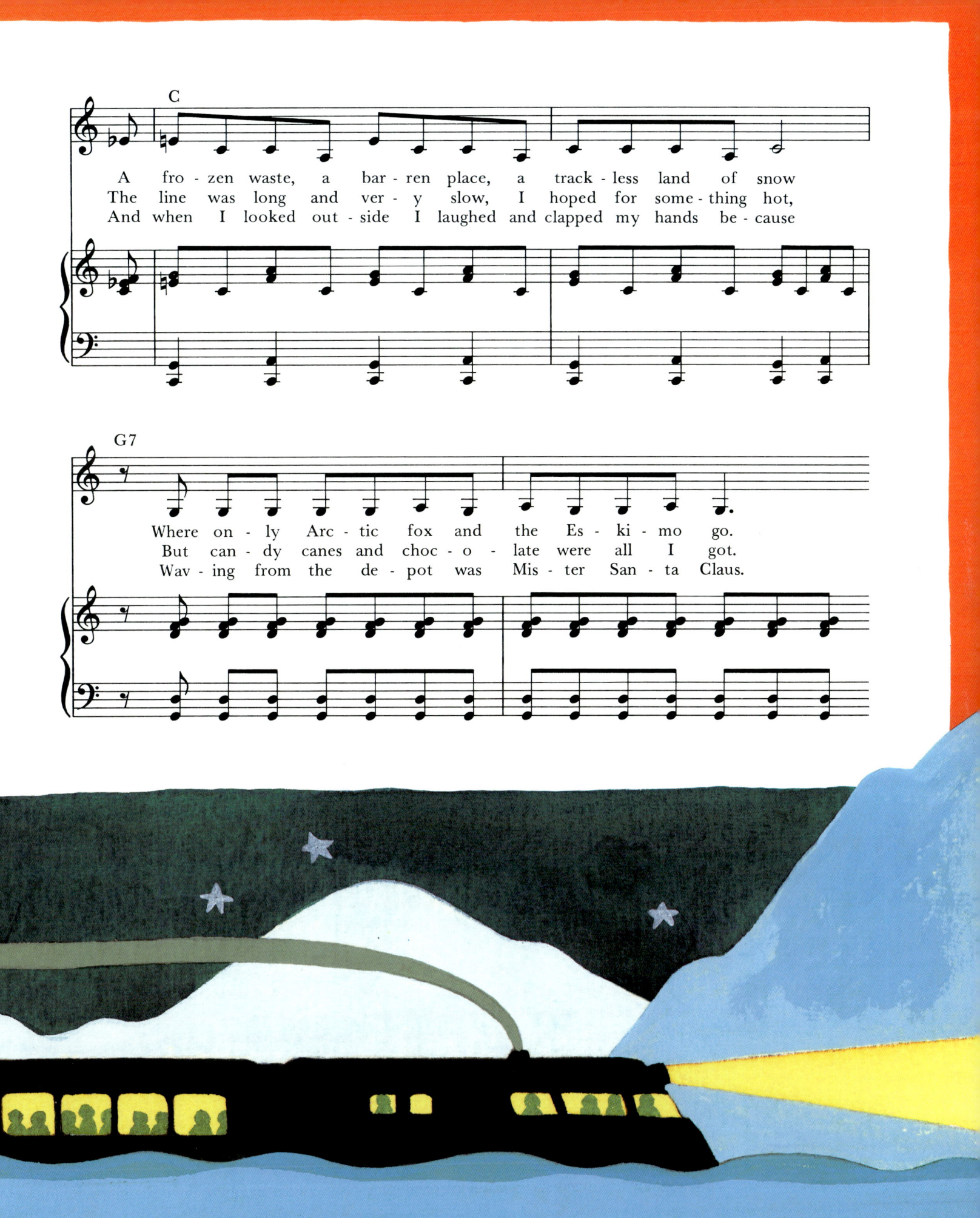

A frozen waste, a barren place, a trackless land of snow
Where only Arctic fox and the Eskimo go.
The line was long and very slow, I hoped for something hot,
But candy canes and chocolate were all I got.
And when I looked outside I laughed and clapped my hands because
Waving from the depot was Mister Santa Claus.

Chorus F7　　　　　　　　　　　　　　　　　　　　　Fm7

The kids who sat a-round me, They were ver-y warm-ly dressed,

C7

With ex-tra socks and all their pock-ets crammed with hand-ker-chiefs.

F7　　　　　　　　　　　　　　　　　　　　　Fm7

It's all a-board, with go-ing for'd In-to the wil-der-ness.

The train pulls from the sta-tion— it's The North Pole Ex-press.

Baboushka

Once long ago in old Russia, in the coldest corner of that cold land, there lived an old woman known as Baboushka. She lived all alone and if she was lonely, she never complained of it, but kept herself busy all day cleaning her house and sleeping the sleep of the just all night.

One morn in the deepest part of the cold winter, just after the longest night, Baboushka was sweeping her steps of a great fall of snow when she saw a strange group of folk riding towards her. The animals they rode on were completely unknown to her; each was larger than a horse, with an odd hump in the middle of its back.

But if she did not know what they rode, she knew the riders. They had to be kings, for they wore crowns of gold and silver. The oldest one wore a crown with a ruby in it the size of a hen's egg. The youngest wore a crown with a sapphire in it the size of a goose egg. And the blackest wore a crown with a diamond in it the size of a fist.

Baboushka made her deepest reverence to them, thinking they would ride on by, for she was but a poor woman and her cottage—though clean—was very small. But they stopped by her door and the beasts they rode made strange *houghing* noises through their noses and one spat at her between its teeth.

"May we stop and sleep the day at your house, Baboushka?" they asked.

She was so awed at the request, she did not wonder they knew her name. But after she had settled them in, all three in her one poor bed, she did begin to wonder for surely honest men worked by day and slept by night, not the other way around. Still when they woke, she did not have the heart to ask them.

It was while she was cooking them dinner, that one—the blackest of the three—told her what she had not dared ask. "We sleep by day and travel by night," he said, "because our way is drawn in the map of the night sky."

When she looked puzzled, he explained that they followed a great star.

"Where do you follow it to?" Baboushka asked.

"To the King of all kings," said the oldest.

"Who is but a newborn babe," said the youngest.

"Come with us this night, Baboushka," they all three said together.

But there was so much to do, cleaning up after the three kings, that Baboushka shook her head. "Let me first sweep up," she said. "I cannot leave my house in such a state."

The kings stood up from the table and looked sadly at her. "We cannot wait, Baboushka. The only road we follow is that outlined by the star. We know not how long the star will shine."

"I will follow as soon as I can," Baboushka said. And she shooed them out the door as if they were chicks and she the mother hen.

The last she saw of them, they were travelling down the road, the great star shining ahead of them and their beasts hawking and spitting as they went.

Baboushka turned back to her little house and began to clean. She swept and she polished and she shook the covers till the down feathers blew about the floor. Then she swept again. By that time, it was nearly dawn and she fell onto her bed and slept.

When she woke and peered outside, the snowfall had covered any tracks, and Baboushka thought it had all been a strange dream.

But by day she cleaned her little house and by night she remembered the kings. She wondered about the little baby who would be King over them all. And the more she wondered, the more she wanted to find Him.

So one day, she cleaned her house for the final time, locked her front door, and started out down the road. Everyone she met she asked about the Baby King, and every baby she saw she peered into the cradle saying, "Are you the One?" In every cradle and in every child's bed she dropped a little gift—just in case it was the very child she sought.

She is still looking.

—adapted from a folk tale from Russia

Jolly Old St. Nicholas

Traditional American carol

Jol - ly old Saint Ni - cho - las, Lean your ear this way!
Don't you tell a sin - gle soul What I'm going to say.
Christ - mas Eve is com - ing soon; Now you dear old man,
Whis - per what you'll bring to me. Tell me if you can.

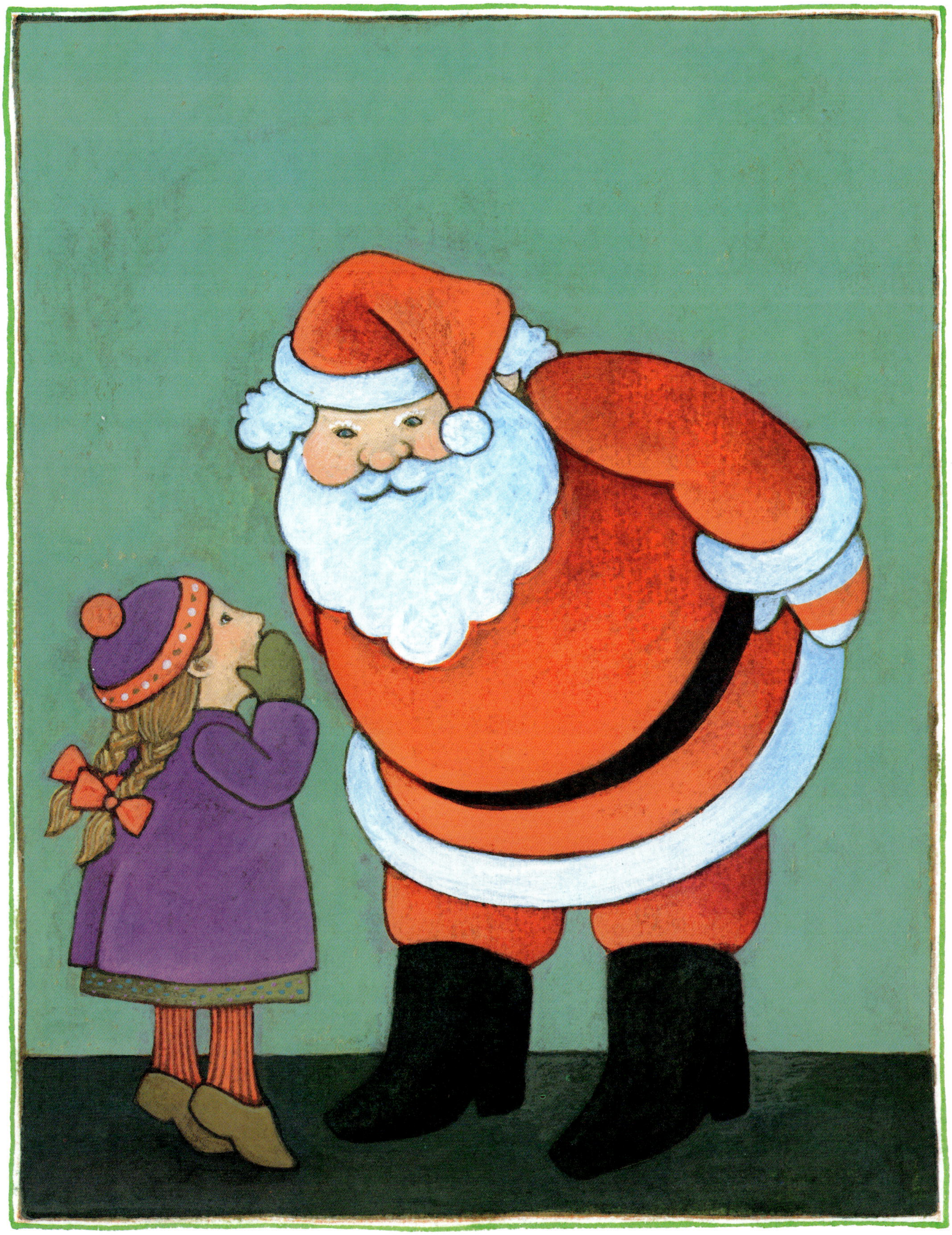

The Christmas Gift

One Christmas morning God was a-walking down the road in Alabama, a-clip, a-clop, a-clip, a-clop, and singing a hymn to himself about how little Baby Jesus had just been born. He was happy and full of all kinds of joy.

Now the Devil was in the neighbourhood, too, out partying too late and much too long. Been drinking up a storm and jumping up a whirlwind and generally up to no good.

When the Devil saw God coming down the road, a-clip, a-clop, a-clip, a-clop, that Devil jumped behind an old stump and hunkered down till nothing showed of him but the tip of his tail and the uppermost part of his left horn. It wasn't that he was scared of God, oh no, but he did want to get himself a Christmas present. He wanted to get—but he didn't want to give. That's the old Devil for you!

So along come God, a-clip, a-clop, a-clip, a—and the Devil jumped up and shouted out "Christmas gift!" 'cause he knew that way God would have to give him something.

—clop. God just went right on walking, and looked over his left shoulder. "You take the East Coast!" he said.

And that's how the East Coast of America got storms and mosquitoes—it's the Devil's property. And there isn't a thing we can do about it 'cause it was a Christmas gift of God's, you see.

—adapted from an African-American folk tale

Santa Rides

What fun to go riding like Santa
In Santa's great reindeer-pulled sleigh,
The snow nicely packed beneath runners
Upon a crisp, bright winter's day.

But what if it's raining or blustery?
Or what if there's hail or there's sleet?
Or worse—if the snow has all melted
And left just a grey city street?

Then Santa will ride in a taxi
Or take a big number ten bus.
But can he go fast without reindeer?
And pack enough presents for us?

Index

BIBLE

And It Came to Pass . . . (Gospel of St Luke), 9

CAROLS

Angels From the Realms of Glory, 104
Boar's Head Carol, The, 88
Carol of the Birds, 50
Come All Ye Shepherds, 22
Deck the Halls, 74
Hark! The Herald Angels Sing, 94
Here We Come A-Wassailing, 84
Holly and the Ivy, The, 68
I Heard the Bells on Christmas Day, 109
Jolly Old Saint Nicholas, 124
Mary Had a Baby, 37
North Pole Express, The, 114
O Christmas Tree, 64
Stable Hymn, The, 57
Twelve Days of Christmas, The, 14
We Three Kings of Orient Are, 26
We Wish You a Merry Christmas, 80

INFORMATION

Animals, Christmas, 38
Carols, Christmas, 90
Food, Christmas, 76
History, A Brief Christmas, 10
Plants, Christmas, 60
Santa Claus and Giving Gifts, 110

PLAY

Foolish Shepherd, The, 96

POEMS

Angel Tunes, 108
Counting Sheep, 20
Donkey's Song, The, 59
Fir Tree, The, 65
Hark!, 5
Legend of Rosemary, The, 73
Paignton Christmas Pudding, The, 86
Praising Cows, The, 42
Santa Rides, 127
Singing Carols, 106
Twelve Pies, 89
We Three Camels, 24
Yule Log, 71

STORIES

Baboushka, 120
Christmas Gift, The, 126
Dough and the Child, The, 82
First Christmas Tree, The, 66
Gift of the Littlest Shepherd, The, 16
Greedy Woman, The, 28
Legend of the Birds, The, 52
Littlest Camel, The, 46
Spider's Christmas Tree, The, 70